The Right Man for the Right Job

The Right Man for the Right Job*

The Executive's Guide to Tapping Top Talent

DR. PHILIP MARVIN
University of Cincinnati

*at the Right Time!

1973
DOW JONES-IRWIN, INC.   Homewood, Illinois   60430

First printing, February 1973

ISBN 0-87094-051-1
Library of Congress Catalog Card No. 72–95404
Printed in the United States of America

To those—
a small select group
who know how to pick
the right man
for the right job
at the right time
and who shared with me
successes,
mistakes made in the past,
and lessons learned from experience.

INTRODUCTION

EVERY ORGANIZATION needs new talent at one time or another. Reasons for shortages include the following:

Growth. The number one cause of manpower shortages arises when organizational activities expand beyond anticipated levels. When these shortages occur, it should be remembered that the planning that misses the highs may also miss the lows.

Failure to Plan. Shortages are inevitable when no attempt is made to anticipate future needs. Change is taking place continually. The only effective way to cope with change is to plan for the future. Failure to plan is to leave things to chance.

Hiring Away. Some men are always "looking" for more money, greater challenge, new geographical locations and the like. These men may be "searched out" by companies with openings to fill. These men should be identified, risks assessed and plans made accordingly. Loss here can be minimized by maintaining salary levels, benefits and opportunities for growth.

Poor Health or Sudden Death. Health and mortality factors are often overlooked in projecting organizational needs. Physical examinations may become perfunctory gestures rather than a basis for planning. Besides, there are the unpredictable events such as heart attacks and accidents to be taken into account.

Failure to Develop Men With Potential. Neglect of promising men is an unnecessary waste of talent that could have satisfied manpower needs.

Initiation of New Activities. New ventures usually create needs for different kinds of talent than those available.

Competitive Pressures. When competitors refurbish their manpower makeup, others who wish to continue to compete also must upgrade the caliber of their manpower cadre.

Early Retirement. When the option is offered, some men elect to opt out.

Failure to Perform. Inability to meet needs may be recognized by the individual or management. In either case, ultimately an opening is created.

Regardless of why a shortage of talent occurs, an executive's most important task is to see that managerial and staff positions are filled. Most of us were not trained to select the right man for the right job. Our skills lie in other fields. Here is a guide to that *critical executive function.* It reflects the best thinking of those who have had a good track record of "wins" in tapping top talent, whether conducting an outside search or promoting from within.

January 1973   PHILIP MARVIN

CONTENTS

Part IV CHECKPOINTS

Part I
Searching

1

DEFINING THE
POSITION TO BE FILLED

"The most prolific area for error is people. I guess over the years I've learned that if I'm 50 percent right, that's a pretty good record. The Peter Principle is absolutely at the top of the list. I hate to tell you how many times I've lost a magnificent salesman and gotten a lousy sales manager, a magnificent engineer and a lousy technical director, a magnificent business unit manager for a stinking group executive, and this goes on and on."*

ED BOOZ, the dean of management counselors once said, "You can reach any goal you want to if you just put the right man on the right job." The soundness of this has been proven time and time again. Yet, managers fail to recognize that they must *search out the right job before they can search out the right man.*

For the manager, defining the job to be done is the first step in searching, screening, and selecting the right man for this

* Rodney Gott, Chairman of AMF Corporation, in an interview in *Business Week*, September 16, 1972.

job, the man through whom the manager will achieve his goal.

All too frequently, a man begins a new assignment only to discover that the job has been oversold, undersold, or otherwise misrepresented by the manager who hired him. J. B., a computer programmer, for example, has changed jobs because he was offered an opportunity to work on complex and sophisticated management information systems. On the new job, J. B. discovered that his predecessor had left because his employer's old-line management thinking wasn't geared to management information concepts.

In another example, Bill was brought into a company to head up a new department to cut production costs and improve manufacturing methods. The division manager had been told by the corporate office to improve his return on investment ratio within two years. On the job, Bill discovered that those responsible for production operations had done an outstanding job. Equipment and processing methods reflected good utilization of latest technologies. Bill also found that losses occurred in raw material purchases. This was an activity outside of his area of authority or special competency. While Bill was more than willing to do what he could, he was unable to act. The Director of Purchases was the division manager's son. The job for which Bill had been hired was not well thought out or workable. It was neither valid nor viable.

J. B. and Bill, as sellers of services, were victims of negligence on the part of the buyers of services who sat on the other side of the bargaining table during the process of searching, screening, and selecting the man for the job. These buyers were negligent in not taking time to define the makeup of the job to be done. When jobs are not well defined, it is not possible to place the right man on the right job.

Managers make this mistake through ignorance. They haven't been trained to search, screen, and select the right man for the right job. Their training has been as applicants for jobs, not as buyers of services. As applicants the job was before them. It didn't need definition. When men become managers, they sometimes are shocked to discover that jobs must be defined.

One reason why job placements of many men are unsuccessful is because managers have failed to define the job to be done. The accepted tool for defining the job is the job description or the position profile. Position profiles are almost universally in bad repute, because managers don't take the time to develop well thought-out working documents.

As a result, most position profiles or job descriptions are vapid showpieces. Only the most naive men take them seriously. The man on the job in many organizations has never seen his job description and if he has seen it he has forgotten it.

Nevertheless, the position profile properly prepared is the working tool of the effective manager. It states what must be done and the problems that must be overcome.

An effective manager spells out long and short range achievements in the position profile. He details what he expects the new man to initiate and follow through to completion. He identifies the roadblocks and frustrations that will be encountered but must be overcome. Beyond this working information, the position profile should delineate responsibilities, the employee's authority to act, his reporting relationships, performance criteria expected and, finally, the organizational "fit."

Those who want to avoid doing their preplacement planning homework argue that these job requirements change with time. But they forget that it is only a working tool for the immediate problem. Let's face a fact. The man you eventually select will not measure up in all respects. His qualifications in some areas may be outstanding but, in other areas weaknesses may exist. Trade-offs most likely will be involved, but without a position profile managers responsible for finding a man for the job will not know how to evaluate any trade-offs. The position profile should be recognized as your working notes that document the demands of the job to be done.

Seven significant factors are involved in preparing a useful position profile:

1. The value added factor
2. The frustration factor
3. The responsibility factor
4. The authority factor
5. The reporting relationship factor
6. The performance criteria factor
7. The fit factor

THE "VALUE ADDED" FACTOR

A manager's first thoughts about the job that must be filled are almost always badly distorted by what has gone before. Take Old Charlie, for example. Old Charlie retired and was replaced, but Old Charlie's replacement isn't carrying his share of the load. "What's wrong?" the manager asks. "We hired a new man, Ted, who matches Old Charlie's capabilities, and he seems to be doing just what Old Charlie always did but Ted doesn't seem to be putting out."

Disturbed by this turn of events, management takes a close look at the situation. The question is now raised: "Is it possible that Old Charlie wasn't doing much of anything himself?" The close look reveals this to be true. Old Charlie had become a fixture not a producer. He had been around for so long it was assumed that he was doing important things.

On the job, Ted, because of his newness, was subject to close scrutiny combined with high expectations. However, his role was complicated by Old Charlie's relative inactivity. Every time Ted made a move to do something, it was questioned because it was a move Old Charlie never made. In fact, Old Charlie made no moves. As a consequence, his replacement must create a new role. In doing so he "makes waves" which disturb others in the organization. Old Charlie never made waves.

In assessing the validity and viability of the action, buyers of services should try to ignore the former incumbent whose job is to be filled and think, rather, about their expectations of the function itself. The controlling question the buyer should ask is, *"During the next year what output from this position would I regard to represent top performance?"*

If buyers of services will think and talk in terms of what they want in the way of output rather than attempting to describe functions, jobs will be better defined.

For example, in hiring J. B., management's expectation of output was the successful implementation of a sophisticated management information system. In terms of expectations, the job wasn't one for a computer programmer. Bill's job wasn't thought through either. The division manager expected an improvement in his return on investment. Nepotism, in the guise of the division manager's son, blocked Bill. Ted's firm was suffering from the old-timer syndrome.

"Value added" should be the controlling criterion in thinking about the services to be bought by the buyer. Let your expectations of an output of specific things that would add up to top performance be the things you are after when you are out to buy services. Nothing else is more important. If, at the end of a year or two, these predetermined outputs are delivered by the chosen one, what else could you want?

Management expectations are less susceptible to distortion when the past record of performance of the man on the job has been good. Top performers make it their responsibility to do what needs to be done. They won't work any way other than the effective way. They will set performance standards for themselves, and they will set these standards at high levels. There is little danger of distortion in basing definitions of future expectations on projections of past performance when top performers retire or leave to accept other positions.

It is not easy to define one's expectations. Many managers don't know what they want. Their hindsight is 20/20; their foresight 20/200. Looking ahead, they can't see beyond today; looking back, they are Monday morning quarterbacks who never called a wrong play. Unless you know what would add up to top performance within the next year or two in the way of performance by the new incumbent in a position to be filled, you are not ready to search, screen, and select the man for the job. The manager who can state his expectations is ready for the second step in documenting the action area.

THE FRUSTRATION FACTOR

The next step in assessing the validity and viability of the action is to identify frustrations associated with the assignment. No job is without attendant frustrations. Buyers of services should identify the frustrations that will confront men on the job. The new men must cope with these job frustrations to act effectively.

Some frustrations are readily recognized. There is rarely enough money available to fund all activities which should be scheduled to do what should be done. This is probably the most frequently encountered frustration that confront men on the job. Yet, the man on the job can't use this as an excuse for failure to perform; he must be able to cope with this frustration.

Buyers of services should size up this situation in advance of searching, screening, and selecting candidates. Buyers should determine when lack of funds will prove to be a major frustration. Unless the underlying factors can be explained to their satisfaction, highly competent men will not accept management's failure to fund programs as other than a reflection of management's lack of interest in them and their particular programs.

Another frustration frequently encountered is that of insufficient manpower of the kind needed to do the job. Few functions are staffed as they should be staffed. It is not just a matter of money, although money plays a big part in the picture. The real culprit is change.

Demands often change faster than manpower moves can be made. The ideal organization man would be capable of doing anything anytime. On the other hand, the specialist or expert can do things that fall within his area of specialization better than the generalist. Competitively, in his area the specialist is in the better posture with respect to quantity, quality, and delivery. A frustration facing the manager is the trade-off he must make between flexibility and productivity.

Then, too, there is the inevitable problem presented by the Old-timers one inherits. Old-timers are neither flexible nor productive, but they are there and will be there until they retire.

A third common frustration arises in the policy area. Rare indeed is the organization that does not have established policies. Policies are governing rules for action. As organizations grow in size, the need for policies increases but policies can and do introduce restraints and rigidity.

Even under the best of conditions, each man can't go his own way without impairing organizational effectiveness; at the same time, operational effectiveness is impaired when men are unduly encumbered by restrictive policies.

Prior to searching for, screening, and selecting the man for the job, you should review policies to identify those which may prove frustrating for the new man. Again, as with money and manpower limitations, time and thought should be given to the need to present policy matters in a manner which will permit men to perform at top levels of effectiveness.

Possibly the greatest of all frustrations is presented by the personalities found in every organization. Some men are chronic empire builders. Others are perfectionists. There are men who are out for a fast buck. And so it goes. The new man must live and work with these people. Buyers of services should identify the problems personalities present.

Added to these frustrations are the ever-present conflicts of interest that exist in every organization. In one sense these conflicts are a sign of good health. The man who doesn't think that the things he is doing are important doesn't do a good job. When each manager wants top priority put on the activities of his group, conflicts arise. But sometimes these conflicts of interest can create difficulties for the new man. For example, if the president's son-in-law heads up a department this can present an additional frustration.

These, then, are just some of the frustrations that a new man can encounter. If they are part of the working milieu, the new man must be able to cope with them to act effectively. Of course, others have survived in the organization despite these frustrations. But these frustrations cannot be wished away. They are there, but they may have become so familiar to members of the existing management group that their impact on the new man is overlooked in assessing the validity and viability of the position to be filled. These frustrations must be identified and documented before management can put the right man in the right job.

THE RESPONSIBILITY FACTOR

At this point, specific performance functions should be itemized. While "value added" should be the controlling criterion in thinking about performance expectations, managers will have other expectations.

For example, one company was searching for a man who, as manager of research and development, could create new products that would add 20 percent in new sales each year beginning with his third year on the job. That is about as specific as one can get in stating a value added expectation.

It might appear that this was about as far as one needed to go in developing working papers for use in searching for the man for the job. Not so.

In thinking about this position, management has determined that there were other duties the new man would be expected to perform. While these were ancillary to developing new products, they also had to be done to support the total activities of the product development division as well as other operations of the company. To be specific, the additional duties were these:

1. Develop corporate policies and objectives that will increase the effectiveness and quality of the research and engineering laboratory operations.

2. Advise general managers regarding the overall level of performance of engineering management in their divisions.

3. Review and recommend approval of the research, product development, and engineering aspects of divisional and subsidiary annual and long-range plans and revisions.

4. Keep appropriate executives informed of technical events and developments within and outside the company which may have a significant effect on the company's plans, programs, and policies.

5. Develop and maintain a corporate technological plan.

6. Provide the following specialized staff services:

a) Maintain a technical liasion service to organize and encourage dissemination of technical information between divisions and between research and the divisions.

b) Stimulate and coordinate the production of articles for professional journals and other outside publications which will reflect and enhance the company's scientific and technical image.

7. Provide patent and idea disclosure liaison between research and product development laboratories and the commercial development staff.

8. Participate with the affected divisions and the commercial development staff in the evaluation of whether the company should obtain a license under the inventions of others.

9. Direct the operation of research laboratories which will supply the fundamental knowledge necessary to provide the corporation with a sound technical base for the development of new products.

10. Review and approve any research activities to be assigned to operating divisions.

11. Review and approve company contractual agreements with government agencies, which relate to research and engineering.

12. Review and recommend action on requests for development of machines or devices for philanthropic purposes.

13. Give advice and counsel in assigned functional areas in such ways as:

a) Provide advice and counsel upon request to division management on scientific and technical matters.

b) Conduct special studies, as requested, on subjects which fall within the scope of the staff's functional responsibilities.

c) Advise operating divisions of factors to be considered in preparation of their annual and long-range plans, and, when requested, give advice in the preparation of these plans.

14. Discharge basic management responsibilities of organizing, staffing, and operating within approved budgetary boundaries in accordance with policies and practices established by the executive committee, to carry out the above duties.

It might appear that these fourteen functions would represent the larger part of the job. Actually, they are parts of the total job that must be done to develop new products. While some of these functions might be of lesser significance than others in the total picture, each plays some part.

Documenting responsibilities to be performed, merely details duties that management thinks are essential for meeting the main or value added expectation. Documenting these in the working papers helps in establishing the validity and viability of the action.

THE AUTHORITY FACTOR

Depending on where the job has been put in the organization chart, the new man's authority to act will vary. In most situations, authority to act can be measured in terms of the dollar budget that can be controlled on a discretionary basis by the man on the job. Simply stated: money speaks louder than words. The man who has money he can spend as he thinks necessary to do what must be done has authority to act.

Of course, this does not tell the whole story of authority. The legal counsel of a company usually has the authority to pass or reject contractural proposals, and control of money is not needed per se. The company recruiter may have the authority to turn away an applicant but no authority to employ a man.

In documenting the position to be filled, management should develop in detail the incumbent's authority to act. Along with this documentation, limitations of authority to act should be detailed for the benefit of all concerned. For example, the man on the job may be permitted to add staff members, as needed, within his budgetary limits but only in accordance with uniform company salary ranges for specific positions. He may be able to authorize purchases below a certain upper dollar limit. Beyond that limit, the approval of his immediate superior may be required. In connection with this common limit to authority, enterprising men have discovered for themselves that when they can't buy the whole because of such rules, they can buy the parts and assemble the whole. Only the less resourceful are restrained from doing what must be done to achieve one's stated goals by such a limitation to their authority to act.

THE REPORTING RELATIONSHIPS FACTOR

Every man reports to someone for something at some time. These reporting relationships aren't always well understood. The working papers used in selecting the man for the job should clarify this relationship.

While in the ideal situation it might be said that a man should report to his immediate superior, and only to him, this is rarely if ever realistic. A man has many bosses, but some men never recognize this fact, and it proves to be their downfall. The position profile should clarify this point to the satisfaction of all concerned.

Inspection of the organization chart clearly reveals that Mr. 2 reports to Mr. 1. Nominally, this is without question. Nominally, Mr. 1 calls the plays and rewards the player who carries, kicks, or tosses the ball as prescribed by Mr. 1 and is, accordingly, rewarded as points are scored in the game. Nominally, that is.

Actually, things rarely work this way. In his machinations and maneuvers, which are part of every man's working day, 2 may foul other players or be fouled by other players or appear to foul other players or appear to be fouled by other players. When this happens, and it will, 2's Mr. 1 begins to hear from the 1s who represent other players. These other 1s are the peers of Mr. 2's boss. Mr. 1 will respond to their views with respect to the performance of his own 2.

Moreover, 2 must support others in his work as well as serve Mr. 1. Favorable comment coming from those 2 supports comes through loud and clear to Mr. 1. In any organization these are powerful voices. Their impact can't be ignored. These voices aren't ignored; they are heard.

Men who have performed the tasks assigned them by the man to whom they report have been defeated by pressures brought to bear by associates antagonized in one way or another by what 2s were doing. Similarly, 1s who were dissatisfied by things 2s were doing have found themselves powerless to remove 2s from the scene of action when 2s were well liked by their associates. In either case, the voices heard come through loud and clear.

This means that before searching for a man for the job, those involved should investigate the informal reporting relationships that will affect the future of the man on the job as much or more than formal reporting relationships. Formal reporting relationships are relatively easy to establish. The detection of informal reporting relationships require a high degree of sensitivity to situations, a degree of sensitivity possessed by only the best of managers.

The detection of these informal reporting relations requires exploration of the intricacies of day to day functional interrelationships. Mr. 2 rarely does any one thing that doesn't have an impact on what someone else is doing. The ideal situation is one in which a man can be all things to all people at all times. It is difficult to do this and do one's own job too. Compromises must be made; risks must be run.

By assessing the need for compromise and the acceptance of risk, requirements can be documented and the priorities to be attached to these requirements can be established. *In some situations, Mr. 2 can do more for Mr. 1 by catering to the needs of others in the organization than he can do for Mr. 1 by catering to Mr. 1's own needs.* It is a wise Mr. 1 who recognizes this situation when it arises.

In documenting reporting relationships, managers are often surprised to discover that it may be more important for a subordinate to be a statesman than an entrepreneur, because only the man who is able to work well with others can do the things he is expected to do. Without the ability to work with others, his efforts are blocked.

In reality, reporting relationships if diagrammed would look more like an organization web than an organization chart. The more complex relationships should be identified and documented in the working papers used in picking the man who can perform on the job.

THE PERFORMANCE CRITERIA FACTOR

The sixth factor to be documented is the performance criteria factor. In part, this is a restatement of the value added factor. In part it is an audit of the wording of the value added factor as well as the responsibility factor.

It should be your *expectation that each man in the organization is going to add something to the organization's overall output that would not be added were that man not part of the organization.* This expectation is not always realized. Too often failure to perform goes unrecognized for long periods of time.

How many times have men retired without being replaced? It was only as old so-and-so was approaching retirement that management, in thinking of his replacement, took enough time to measure the value added factor only to discover that old so-and-so had added no value for as far back as anyone can remember.

How many times when men have gone on extended sick leave has it been discovered that the organization's output hasn't fallen? Even worse, how many times has output risen? Again here is prima facie evidence suggesting that someone did not contribute added value to the organization's output.

The purpose of the performance criteria factor is to reduce this risk. It calls to the attention of the manager and the candidates the fact that performance on the job is measurable. This fact should also have been incorporated in the documented statement of value added.

For example, in the case of the search for a manager of research and development, the value added contribution of the man selected was expected to consist of a continuing series of new products that would add 20 percent in new sales each year commencing the third year the man was on the job. In itemizing performance criteria, no more than that need be said. It is a clear, concise, and measurable statement of value added expectation.

In another situation, in searching for a sales manager, performance was to be measured on the basis of the sales manager's ability to produce sales by market areas that met quotas established by a market research group reporting to the financial vice president. A production manager who could cut costs 12 percent was the subject of another search. In this situation it was made clear that he couldn't cut costs by reducing quality. Quality control reported to the vice president for engineering, not the production manager.

Restatements of value added expectations should head up the listing of performance criteria. To the degree that expectations can be expressed in finite numbers to that same degree men's goals will be made more specific and challenging. Statement of criteria in finite numbers is not always possible. Some criteria can be expressed only in relative terms.

For example, a performance criterion stated as "establish a leadership position in the market place" can be measured only in relative terms. The job of establishing a leadership position depends on the competition. It is easier to be No. 1 in the market place if No. 2 doesn't try too hard.

Words like capable, significant, imaginative, adequate, competent, awareness, promptness, and soundness are not very useful in stating a performance criterion.

In the case of the search for the manager of research and product development the performance criteria were stated as follows:

1. Development of new products that add an additional 20 percent in new sales each year commencing within a three year period.
2. Ability of the research laboratories to provide significant fundamental information for product development.
3. Imagination in defining objectives, anticipating future requirements, and guiding the direction of forward planning.
4. Adequacy of corporate policies and plans developed.
5. Awareness of new techniques and devices relating to his specialized area.
6. Competence and promptness in rendering specialized services to corporate and division managements.
7. Soundness of advice and counsel furnished.

These statements encompass both finite and relative performance criteria. Performance criteria should always relate and reflect stated value added expectations as well as responsibility criteria. Statements of performance criteria should not introduce expectations and responsibilities unrelated to those previously documented in the position profile.

THE FIT FACTOR

The chief executive of a firm that enjoys international renown points out that a man's success in any situation is due not only to his ability to perform but to what this executive calls body chemistry. He has found in his long and extensive experience that body chemistry accounts for 50 percent of the makeup of a man's success on the job.

Few seasoned executives will deny the need to fit the man to the temperament, geography, and social makeup surrounding the situation for which he may be considered. Every situation is different. Some men can work in almost any environment. Other men who are top performers working in one environment, figuratively fall apart in another environment. For example, in some positions in New York City and other cities, a two or three martini lunch is part of the job. Long commuting trips daily can't be avoided by the man who wants to enjoy suburban living.

Not only are such externals brought into the picture in determining the degree to which a man fits into the scene of action but *internal customs* also come into play. No one can deny the enormous success of IBM. In all probability, without Thomas J. Watson, Sr., there would be no IBM today. It may be that much of today's cohesiveness in the IBM organization has been due to IBM's songbook. Certainly, over the years, competitors lacking a songbook were less successful.

Notwithstanding, not every man is geared to singing such songs as IBM's immortal "Ever Onward," the verse and choruses of which are here preserved.

EVER ONWARD

There's a thrill in store for all,
For we're about to toast
The Corporation in every land.
We're here to cheer each pioneer
And also proudly boast
Of that "man of men," our friend and guiding hand.
The name of T. J. Watson means a courage none can stem:
And we feel honored to be here to toast the "IBM."

Chorus

EVER ONWARD—EVER ONWARD!
That's the spirit that has brought us fame!
We're big, but bigger we will be,
We can't fail for all can see
That to serve humanity has been our aim!
Our products now are known in every zone.
Our reputation sparkles like a gem!

We've fought ourway through—and new
Fields we're sure to conquer too
For the E V E R   O N W A R D   I B M.

Second Chorus

EVER ONWARD—EVER ONWARD!
We're bound for the top never to fall!
Right here and now we thankfully
Pledge sincerest loyalty
To the corporation that's the best for all!
Our leaders we revere, and while we're here
Let's show the world just what we thing of them!
So let us sing, men! SING, MEN!
Once or twice then sing again
For the E V E R   O N W A R D   I B M.

Singing songs may be *de trop* in IBM today but not every company has given up its inspirational songs. The aim and objective of the fit factor is to bring together people who share in common specific likes and dislikes. Once brought together these individuals work together and stay together. Men who sing together may stick together, but not everyone wants to sing.

In other firms, everything from country clubs at one end of the social scale to pheasant hunting, pitching horseshoes, bowling, and poker play a part in the makeup of the fit factors. Depending on the situation, a man may be made or broken by his participation or reaction to *functional nonessentials*.

Another aspect of fit is management temperament. Some firms are made up of high pressure performers. It has never been proven that this breed of man accomplishes more or even as much as those whose pace is slower. However, the high pressure man can't work well with those whose pace is slower. The slow mover isn't accepted in the fast moving, high pressure melee and the high pressure man's competence is questioned by the slower moving Brahmin.

One must consider the wife's role at this point, too. Is she expected to be a company wife, to push her husband, or to play a passive role? One organization tries to make a man's wife unhappy with her lot in life in order to prompt her to encourage her husband to work harder and earn more money. A wife's activities in the women's club may be a major determinant of a man's future. In other companies a man's wife may become unhappy when she discovers that she is not a part of the company's activities. Any efforts on her part to inject herself into company affairs may have a negative effect on her husband's future.

Another facet of the fit factor to be considered is that of geography. Some like it hot and some like it cold. Some like the big city and some like the small town. Some like the mountains and some like the seashore.

Along with the geographic facet of fit there is an identity facet. Some like to be identified with science-oriented organizations, such as electronic, space, or chemical companies. These men would be unhappy in companies that produce earth-moving machinery or typewriters. Others want to be identified with the financial community, welfare, or insurance. Then there are those who want to be part of "bigness" while others want to be big frogs in small puddles. Growth situations, similarly, have an allure for one man while another identifies with stability and tradition.

Inscribed upon the shrine of the Delphic Oracle are the words: Know thyself. In documenting working papers to be used in picking your man for the job, you must know your organization and what it will take for others to fit into it.

There isn't any right or wrong attached to the myriad facets of fit but there is a difference between fit and failure to fit. Those documenting the position profile should know what it takes to fit. One can't pick the man that will fit the situation without identifying operative facets of the fit factor.

Among manpower recruiters the thing that distinguishes the professional from the amateur is the former's well-thought-out and well-documented position profile. He has in hand the design specifications needed to pick the man for the job. The amateur, having neglected his homework, can only eliminate the obviously unfit and gamble on the remaining candidates.

The position profile should *detail the makeup of the man the organization can digest and who, in turn, can digest the organization.* Not everyone who would be satisfactory to the group finds the group satisfactory to him.

2

PROSPECTING FOR PROSPECTS

INEXPERIENCED MANAGERS faced with the problem of filling positions in their organizations make a common mistake of trying to ride off in all directions at once. Authorized to add a man to their group they let it be known that they have an opening and commence interviewing applicants without taking time to plan any search strategy. As a consequence, while they may end up with a man who can do a job they rarely end up with the man who can do the best job.

For example, Fred, a manufacturing manager, decided to add a value analysis expert to his staff. Fred wasn't certain in his own mind just what such a man would do, but he felt he would get a fix on the position while he was talking to the candidates. Fred let it be known around the company that he was looking for such a man, and at the same time he placed an advertisement in a local paper with a good circulation in a heavily industrialized area.

The response was overwhelming. Fred got over two hundred letters. His home telephone rang all weekend. For a full week, his working time was taken up with talking with applicants. Finally on Friday, a week after the advertisement first appeared, Fred found a man, Ralph, who appeared to know what he was talking about. After a telephone check with two of Ralph's references, Ralph was hired. With a sigh of relief, Fred told the rest of the applicants that the opening was filled.

In one sense, Fred's experience had a happier ending than others who made the same mistakes Fred made. Ralph was interested in value engineering and willing to learn the job. He had heard a talk on value engineering at the engineer's club and it sounded like interesting work. He had been frank in presenting his capabilities to Fred at the time of his interview. Fred was impressed by Ralph's candor and willingness to accept the challenge offered by the position. On the job, Ralph worked hard. He took an evening course in value engineering and applied himself to his work during the day. Fred was happy. Ralph was happy.

Finding fault with his success story seems like looking for trouble just to make trouble, but not so. From any objective management viewpoint, Fred missed by a mile. To go back to the beginning, Fred sensed an opportunity to improve his operating effectiveness through utilization of value analysis techniques about which, admittedly, he knew nothing. Fred decided to add a value analysis expert to his staff, but he didn't follow through. In hiring Ralph, Fred hired a trainee, not an expert. Fred set up a training program to train a man in an area outside of his own competency. Fred did not add expertise to his staff; he merely added a man who was willing to learn.

Fred did not achieve his objective in hiring Ralph. Fred, like many other men, got sidetracked because he tried to do too many things at one time. He tried to search, screen, and select all at the same time without developing any well-thought-out strategies or tactics.

The search for candidates is a job that can't be slighted or combined with screening. Until a search is satisfactorily completed, nothing else should be done. No attempt should be made to screen candidates until one is satisfied that the most likely candidates have been corralled.

Remember, if a potentially top performer is missed during the search his name won't appear in the final list of candidates to be considered in selecting the man for the job. Put another way, if the man who would have been the best man to fill the opening is overlooked during the search for candidates, the best man can't be selected. A second best man must be chosen. The competence with which the search is conducted controls the level of competence of candidates from which final selections are made.

FOCUS ON FUNCTION

In initiating any search the focus is on function. The buyer's objective is to identify the men who are already doing outstanding jobs in the area of need. Forget, for the time being, any thoughts of potential; look for performance. Later, if necessary, you may lower your sights and begin looking for less, because no top-level man is available. As a result, you must hire on hopes of performance rather than on proof of performance. However, there is no rational reason for searching for potential rather than performance at the outset. Simply stated, search out the men who are already doing an outstanding job in what is wanted.

In looking for a manufacturing manager, you start out by identifying men who are already performing the functions the new man will be called upon to perform. Regardless of the nature of the position to be filled, president, nursing supervisor, librarian, company physician, or corporation legal counsel, look for the man who is already doing an outstanding job of performing in the position to be filled. The best proof of a man's ability to perform at top levels is his performance at top levels.

By this time someone is sure to be wondering why the candidate list shouldn't include men who possess potential to perform but who are not, as yet, performing the specific functions of immediate interest. The scope of the search should be defined by the position profile. If a top performer is needed, the search should limit itself to proven performers. When a less than top performer will meet these requirements, this should be spelled out in the position profile.

For example, in filling an opening for a corporate counsel, the position profile may state alternatives. A lawyer, well experienced in corporate work who will, himself, perform the corporation's case work load may be one alternative identified in the profile. In another alternative, an inexperienced man would develop his skills through practice but would initially serve in a liaison capacity between the corporate officers and a law firm. Here the search should look for competence, on the one hand, and potential, on the other hand. In every respect, two searches are being conducted. Two groups of candidates should be corralled.

The well-thought-out profile defines the function. Where trainees will be tolerated in place of proven performers, this should be so stated. The position profile determines needs. Once needs have been defined, the search should be limited to the identification of qualified candidates.

CORRALLING CANDIDATES

The questions a manager asks himself at this point are "How do I find the men who are top performers? Who and where are the men who are doing an outstanding job doing the things I want done?" Answering this question isn't an easy task.

Those responsible for conducting searches should set aside adequate time in their schedules to do this job as it should be done. Even if a manager has candidates in mind, he should search for even better qualified candidates before making any attempt to select a man to fill the opening. The best qualified man known to a manager may not be the best qualified man for the job. Unless a manager is willing to take the time and make a search for the best qualified candidates, he limits his selection to a second best field of candidates. As a consequence, his final selection can't be better than second best.

Now to the questions. "Who and where are the candidates?" They are on the job somewhere doing what he wants done. All that he has to do is to identify the places where these functions are performed. This can be done, but it takes time. It is not easy, but the way in which to identify these men is an easily plotted pathway.

Before looking outside for candidates, an in-house search should be conducted. Armed with a position profile, no difficulty should be experienced in identifying positions that match the profile. For the time being, all men filling these positions should be regarded as candidates. Questions as to their availability should be left until later. In smaller organizations, the in-house search for these men is easier than in larger organizations. In large organizations, divisions and subsidiaries may be so numerous, unfamiliar, and inaccessible that they must be covered in a synoptic search.

The synoptic search is the everywhere search. That is, it is a search directed at every position wherein a man is performing the functions prescribed in the position profile. While the synoptic approach is an everywhere approach in concept, such restraints as time, technology, size, level of position, size of operation, and funding available for the search are introduced. Compromise is inevitable.

Compromises that come into play in conducting the search

depend on the function to be filled. For example, the level of the position within the organizational hierarchy frequently results in compromises with respect to the scope of the search. A search for a president may be conducted on a national scale, whereas a search for a machine shop foreman is localized.

Another compromise arises as a result of organizational size and complexity. Large corporations recruit nationally as a general practice. The smaller the organization the more localized are its recruiting practices. For example, a large corporation looks for engineers on a wider scale than a smaller organization looking for a vice president.

Limited availability of a technical specialty may require yet another compromise. A search for a supervisor of crystal production, a glass blower, a laser expert, or a man to program machine tools would be conducted on a national scale. These men are scarce. On the other hand, a search for a company physician or legal counsel is commonly limited to the local area.

A wide scale search takes longer than a local area search and costs more. Compromises made reflect restraints imposed by what are believed to be practical considerations. In effect, management says to itself, by searching farther we might do a little better in corralling candidates but not enough better to justify the time, effort, and cost. This is a judgmental matter but reflects, nonetheless, compromises with performance.

Management can be expected to be found later making similar mistakes in the course of conducting subsequent searches for prospects for other positions. Only by following a well-worked-out strategy with planned tactics can mistakes be avoided. Any compromise affects performance levels. The broader the scope of the search, the greater is the probability of making the best candidates available for the purpose of picking the man for the job.

THE SYNOPTIC SEARCH

In zeroing in on prospective candidates, ask for advice and suggestions. Seek out someone in a key spot, a man on the job or a job closely related to the functional area of the search.

For example, in one effort to find a director of research for a pharmaceutical house, the first step was to identify the men who were doing an outstanding job in this position. Annual reports of selected pharmaceutical companies were reviewed to learn the names of research executives. Some were telephoned; others were written to. They were told of the opening. An appointment was sought to visit each of them for the purpose of getting advice as to where the man wanted may be found.

Approached in the proper manner, most men are willing to offer their advice and counsel. In initiating a search, one needs to track down the names of outstanding prospects. Ask those contacted at the outset about the availability of directories of people working in the pertinent functional areas and, in particular, ask for the names of the individuals considered to be outstanding performers as well as suggested candidates for the position. One may be in for a surprise; men contacted often throw their hat in the ring and become candidates. They have nothing to lose, and there may be something to be gained.

During one initial discussion with a controller for the purpose of developing a prospect list, a discussion between the president seeking a controller and the controller in another company proceeded along these lines:

PRESIDENT: I appreciate your taking time to talk with me. Our controller was killed in an automobile accident and the man who might have replaced him became a group executive a short while back. We don't want to move him again so soon. Now we must look outside. The question is where to start. It occurred to me that you might have some thoughts to offer about men who could suggest some candidates or some suggestions as to men you know who would be likely prospects.

CONTROLLER: I'd be glad to do what I can. We all face unantici-pated needs from time to time. Of course, all of the controllers of any consequence belong to one or two financial groups. I'll let you borrow my copy of the directory of the Financial Executives Institute. It lists men in key spots.

PRESIDENT: Would you care to pinpoint any of these men as men whose counsel I should seek. I'm looking for a top man and am willing to pay what it takes to attract him.

CONTROLLER: Well, yes, there are several. Here, let me check them off. By the way, we are involved in a merger. If I accept the position which has already been offered me as controller of the new combina-tion, it will be necessary for me to move from here to the new cor-porate office in Chicago. Since I am going to have to consider that move I might be interested in talking with you at greater length about your opening.

PRESIDENT: I'd be delighted to explore this with you. Let me call you and set a date for luncheon some noon.

Right from the start in zeroing in on prospects when you are talking with those in functional areas of interest you will find that these men become prospects themselves. Why shouldn't they? Why should any man pass up an opportunity to get his name on a prospect list for a potentially promising opportunity?

The searcher, however, should be looking for leads as well as prospects themselves. He should concentrate on widening the scope of the search. It is a mistake to get sidetracked from the main purpose of developing leads at the outset of the search.

In addition to talking with those one already knows and following up worthwhile leads developing from this source, a second tool to use in zeroing in on candidates is the direc-tory of a trade or professional association representing func-tional areas of interest.

For example, if the search is for a microscopist for a milling company laboratory, the directory of the American Associa-tion of Feed Microscopists is a prospect list in itself. There are over 4,300 national trade and professional associations. Most functions men perform are represented by more than one association. To illustrate, a geologist may belong to any one of 17 associations for geologists and his name may show up in other associations in peripheral areas.

Another source of prospects is developed through advertisements in publications such as *The Wall Street Journal,* local newspapers, and the publications of associations. When advertising, give the company name and the name of a man to contact. When it is necessary to keep the search a secret from those in the company, a box number can be used in advertisements. Whenever possible this should be avoided. Good men are reluctant to respond to blind advertisements. They won't know who they are telling of their interest in a move. They might be responding to their immediate superiors.

The most productive source of top-level prospects is through direct contact by telephone or better by letter and, even better still, by personal visit. Call, write, or visit those in the know. Tell them of the need. Ask for the names of individuals recommended for the job not for the names of men looking for a job.

While men who are unemployed or openly seeking a new job should not be overlooked, this group of prospects always contains a higher proportion of men who, for one reason or another will be rejected in the screening process for the same reasons that have been the underlying cause of their present search for a new position. The best prospect list proves to consist of men on the job who are performing at top levels. These men can be contacted only by personal telephone call, letter, or visit.

Ask these men for the names of those they think can fill the position described to them. Answer their questions. Listen to their answers. Ask them if they can be reached again for further advice later.

Create an opportunity for the man to volunteer his interest

in becoming a prospect by telling him that he is the kind of man needed, if such is the case. Ask him if he would consider the position. If so, ask him if he has a résumé. Most men have résumés. Résumés serve a variety of useful purposes such as introductions when they give talks or editorial use when they write articles.

In the event that a man doesn't commit himself, drop the subject. His interest can be explored later. Add his name to the prospect list for further study, if he appears to be the kind of man who might be well qualified for the job.

Discussion up to this point has centered on corralling candidates for positions demanding identifiable expertise. The search has been for men performing specific functions. Now, how about picking men to move in at lower organizational levels who have the capability to move up?

SEARCHING OUT THE BEGINNERS

The men just starting out fall into two groupings of prospects. In the first group there is the graduating senior. In the second group there is the man who has been on a job from two to four years.

In developing prospects for positions for which men in these two groupings qualify, some feel that these men represent an exception to the rule that a search should be made for performers. It is argued that these men have not had an opportunity to perform. This argument results from confusing performance with expertise.

The beginner may not have developed identifiable expertise but he has been doing things in a competitive frame of reference even while in school. The search for prospects in these groupings should be conducted on the same basis as any other search.

With respect to the graduating senior, start with the department of the college from which the prospect would logically graduate. For example, in searching for an accounting graduate, talk with some accounting firms. Learn the names of schools that have outstanding, not just accredited but outstanding, faculties that have been turning out performers. Invite the department head and a few of his senior faculty members to a luncheon. Tell them of specific interests and ask the names of students who have been top performers in the classroom.

In doing this don't be afraid to travel. Nearby schools may have a weak faculty in a particular field of interest. No college or university regardless of its public image has a top quality faculty in every department. In conducting a search for graduates, judge departments, not colleges or universities.

Searching out the man who has been on the job two to four years is the most difficult of all searches to conduct on a man to man basis. These men have had little opportunity to establish the contacts that they will have developed by the time they have been working five years or more.

Many of the better men and the more aggressive of the men will have joined a professional organization or two. Through the members of local chapters of national associations these men can be identified. Others will be visible as a result of having participated in church and civic affairs. Those who are taking graduate evening courses or teaching these courses can be identified, too.

The "lost" man for purposes of the search may be the man whose job takes up all of his time and who is known only to a few close associates and his superior. Superiors, when contacted, won't recommend their own top performers as prospects for a raid on talent unless they have a surfeit of top talent or budget cuts are scheduled. The only way the names of these men will surface is when a peer suggests an associate he would like to see move out to clear the way for his own move up.

In searching for prospects in these two groupings, the men of interest are those who have performed tasks which they have been assigned. Few can establish identifiable expertise within the first few years of graduation but men have the opportunity to prove their ability to perform on assigned tasks from the time they first enter school. The search should identify these performers. Performers are prospects.

Since each man with whom one talks during the development of prospects is a link with a recommended prospect and is often a prospect himself, it is worthwhile to make some notes about the man with whom one has talked. These notes should take shape as answers to six questions.

Does he know the men in his field? A good clue to a man's level of competence is his awareness and knowledge of his peers. The man who doesn't know what others are doing doesn't know what's going on in his functional specialty. One can't know what's going on without knowing who is doing what. When one knows who is doing what, one knows the names of these people.

Watch for the man who fumbles for names. At the same time one should be aware that some men follow a practice of appearing to be ignorant or temporarily forgetful to give themselves time to size up a situation before making commitments. It is an effective and artful dodge much like that employed by the slow thinker who hides this commonly encountered weakness behind the puffing on a pipe or the lighting of a cigar. Other men may be reluctant to suggest candidates without first talking with the men to be recommended.

Is he credible? In other words, does he appear to know what he is talking about? Remember, at this point one is recording impressions. Impressions are not researched facts, but it is important to know whether a man conducts himself in a way which conveys competence or incompetence. Regrettably, there are those of little real competence who can put their ideas across better than those of far greater competence.

The shadier the scheme one is selling the greater must be one's skill in conveying credibility. The great con men of all time have been the most believable of men as they sold such things as shares in ventures that ended in bankruptcy or building lots located under a lake. Other men, highly competent in their work, have a demeanor which fails to convey credibility. They may be hesitant, withdrawn, equivocating or reticent in their remarks. Regardless of the fact that they are right in the things they do and say, they don't convey credibility. It is only through long and close association with these men that one becomes aware of their competence.

The con man and the introvert expert reflect two extremes. Most men convey a degree of competence through their general demeanor that reflects reality. A first impression as to the degree to which this is achieved should be noted.

Was he articulate? Does he express himself clearly and concisely or must one repeatedly rephrase questions to get to answers? One knows he knows but it is difficult to understand what he is saying.

Some men have the ability to choose words that tell the story. Abstract ideas are made simple by the selection of examples or by the drawing word pictures. One suspects that others are deliberately difficult to understand in order to cloak their own incompetence and lack of understanding.

Does he listen? Some men spend so much time talking they never learn what is going on. Others just don't hear what is being said.

When one can't squeeze one's questions or remarks into the conversation, a nonlistener has been encountered. When answers to questions aren't answers to the question asked, one is usually talking to a nonlistener. The listener creates a climate for conversation; others are encouraged and permitted to hold the floor. Their questions are often answered by questions to give them a greater opportunity to express their viewpoint.

Does he convey a sense of purpose? Does he know what he is doing and where he is going? Some do, most don't. Ask the man on the move about some problem or opportunity in his area of expertise. He will tell you about his plans to act or not to act and the basis for his decision. The man on the move is not a man watching from the sidelines. He is involved in the action. He knows why he is involved and where he wants to go.

The men who are watching things happen and wondering why they are happening or don't know things have happened haven't established a place for themselves. Things are happening to these men. They aren't making things happen. They aren't in command. In fact, they won't take command or accept command.

Does he create a favorable impression? This in an overview question. Affirmative answers to the preceding five questions are almost certain to anticipate an affirmative answer to this question, too. However a man may know the men in his field, exude credibility, express himself loud and clear, listen well, be achievement oriented, and put one off rather than create a favorable impression. A man can be domineering, self-centered, or create an unfavorable impression for other reasons.

Another man may have charisma and little else to offer. There are those who have an incredible personal magnetism and no other personal asset. Even though they are saying nothing that makes sense, one listens spellbound. In these cases, five negative answers are followed by an affirmative notation.

THE PROSPECT LIST

The important end product of the search is a prospect list. If the prospect list develops candidates, one of whom is selected and accepts the position, the search is over. If not, the search must be resumed. Time should be taken to do this job properly. Valuable time is lost when searches must be reactivated because the right man hasn't been found the first time around.

Part II
Screening

3

RESEARCHING THE RECORD

PROSPECTING FOR potential candidates ends when diligent search has revealed the men who are doing outstanding jobs in the position that is the subject of the search. There is no formula that can be applied to tell when a sufficient number of men have been identified. Experience is the best teacher, but one should have a feeling of assurance that one has identified the top performers.

One can never identify all of the possible prospects for any position. However, one should be sure that a sufficient number of prospects have been selected to assure a reasonable probability that a man can be found who will accept the position. To repeat: Experience is the best teacher; there is no formula that can be substituted for experience.

All that is known up to this point about these men is that they appear to be outstanding performers in the functional area of interest. In zeroing in on the man for the job, one must first eliminate those whose experience, performance, or makeup eliminates them as candidates for the opening for which the search is being conducted.

Some of these men will have been recommended because they were friends of friends. Others will have had an outstanding record due to circumstances beyond their control rather than personal ability. A man may have looked good during a period of prosperity and expansion which concealed his mediocre performance and poor judgment. There will be those whose popularity flows from personality or conviviality. Along with all of these men there will be top performers. The task at this point is to determine who's who.

The prospect list has been built up in a number of ways. Word-of-mouth announcement of an opening, when openings are made known to others this way, will have brought doorknockers, men with résumés. Advertisements carrying in the copy a company name will have produced more doorknockers and résumés. Blind ads will have produced a flow of letters accompanied by résumés. Personal visitation and telephone solicitation of prospects will have produced names along with an occasional résumé.

While the searcher regards these men as prospects at this point in time, many will not survive the elimination process and others will not want to be considered for the position. The doorknockers have signaled their initial interest in the position by their letters and résumés. Others, when approached, acknowledged an interest. Still others are as yet only names. Not having been contacted, these men are unknowns insofar as their interest in the position is concerned. The next job is to learn more about these men.

Prospects should be communicated with in much the same manner as was followed in developing the initial prospect list itself. The prospect should be approached obliquely. Call him for an appointment. Don't ask him if he would be interested in the job, tell him of your interest in locating an outstanding man to do a job and describe the job. Get him talking about possible candidates. Ask him about his work and the things he has been able to accomplish in the past. Show an interest in his activities. Ask him if he finds that his assignment gives him ample opportunity to make full use of his talents. Tell him he looks like the type of man who should be considered for the opening under study. Ask him if he would be willing to be a candidate and ask him for a résumé. Such a conversation would customarily follow the pattern of the conversation between Jack, who was conducting a search and Ken, a prospect on Jack's list.

JACK: I appreciate your willingness to take time to talk with me. I'm looking for a highly qualified man to head up a marketing research group for a multidivisional corporation, one of the top 100 in *Fortune's* 500 list. The salary is open. The man for the job is the man who can manage a research group that will come up with answers. His performance will be based on the rightness of the answers. He's got to produce.

KEN: Others help me when I am looking for an outside opinion. I'm glad to be able to help, too, when I can, but I'm not sure that I'll be able to come up with some names without giving the matter some thought.

JACK: No, of course not, but you've been in this business a long time, and few others would know people like you do.

KEN: Well, I have been engaged in marketing research for some time, but not everyone works my way.

JACK: You have been highly successful with a number of innovations, haven't you?

KEN: Thanks, I'm always grateful for a word of praise. Much of the success of my group is due to our bringing together marketing, technology, and sales thinking in our findings. My experience suggests that you can't isolate marketing research and come up with answers that are worth anything.

JACK: Our management thinks this way, too. The problem is to find a man who can get a group of tigers to work together. How do you do it?

KEN: Remember, these people all report to me. Answers that direct corporate product programs are their first and only responsibility. Men see things differently when they don't have three separate reporting relationships.

JACK: But you inject something into this, too, I know.

KEN: I act as an arbitrator but, more importantly, I try to anticipate conflicts in points of view and maintain a climate conducive to cohesive thinking.

JACK: You make it sound easy but I know that's because you are a real pro. The pro always makes things look easy. He's had the practice that accompanies experience.

KEN: It does get easier as time passes but, then, if problems get bigger and bigger all of the time, the job gets more challenging.

JACK: Is that happening here? Do you find enough expansion and growth to give you ample opportunity to make full use of your talents?

KEN: Not always but, then, I'm impatient. I like to do big things.

JACK: If I could prove to your satisfaction that the position I'm talking about provided those opportunities, would you be willing to explore the opening?

KEN: I hadn't thought about me for the position but why not. If you will keep the matter confidential, you can think about me. I'm not looking. I'm happy here but shouldn't every man have a price on his head?

JACK: When you give a talk or write an article you must have some biographical data you make available to the program chairman or editor, how about letting me have a copy.

KEN: Be glad to. My secretary has a file folder full of them. I'll get you one.

JACK: I'll get back to you shortly. In the meantime I'll read over your biographical material. Again, thanks for the time you've given me.

KEN: It was my pleasure.

Jack left without having received suggestions from Ken with regard to prospects for the position but Jack had what he wanted, an indication from Ken that he was willing to be considered a candidate. Jack also left with a copy of Ken's biographical data. Jack was satisfied. He had used the prospect ploy at this point merely to gain access to Ken.

THE PROSPECT PARADOX

Many men are confused by a seemingly contradictory or inconsistent aspect arising between the development of a prospect list and the interviewing of prospects. These men ask, "Why is the approach to men the same in both cases?"

The reason is the fact that in developing a prospect list the approach is a direct one for that purpose. In seeking out prospects themselves, an indirect approach is more effective and safer for the prospect.

A man's relationship with his employer may be compromised if it becomes known that he is being considered for another position even though he played no part in initiating his candidacy. Moreover, to approach a man and ask him if he is willing to be a candidate for a job without giving him time to adjust his thinking to the situation is just poor practice.

The best approach to a prospect is to get him thinking about the opening as well as the makeup of men who might qualify by asking him to suggest prospects. The basic difference between this situation and the earlier situation in which prospects are being identified is that this man is the prospect. In the earlier situation, the man involved was contacted because he was in a position to help identify prospects. He might be a potential prospect himself or he might be someone in an indirectly related situation such as a banker, lawyer, or more senior executive. He is selected as a source rather than a prospect although he may be both.

There is another aspect of the prospect paradox that it is important to understand. Men should remain on the prospect list even though they say they are not interested in being considered a candidate. The fact that a man indicates a lack of interest should be noted. However, someone pointed to these men as men who do outstanding jobs. One mustn't lose sight of the fact that further study may reveal one of these men to be the best man for the job. If so, one should go back and ask that man to reconsider. He may refuse a second time, but it is worth the effort. The objective is to put the best man on the job.

At the completion of this first go-around you should have prospects classified in two groups: announced candidates who have made biographical data available and the no-candidate group that has not made biographical data available. Prior to this point a number of the prospects were unannounced candidates. They were not aware that they were under consideration. Now all the candidates are either announced candidates or are in the no-candidate group. Those in the first group will cooperate in the further selection of a final candidate. If a background check is desired in the no-candidate group it will be necessary to pursue this without the cooperation of the individual involved. He has said he has no interest in the position.

POSITIONING PRIORITIES

Once announced candidates and no-candidates have been separated, the time comes to set some priorities. Time is always a scarce resource. First things must be put first. Judgmental decisions must be made. The most likely candidates should receive first attention. In so doing, three things come into play: the position profile, the sponsor's credibility, and the candidate's profile revealed by resumes and biographical data.

Even if there was ample time to explore in breadth and depth the qualifications of each prospect, one would need to start with some one candidate. As a group the more promising prospects are the announced candidates. These men include those who have either volunteered by responding to advertisements or have indicated an interest in the position following sponsorship of their names by others who were asked to suggest the names of top performers. Résumés or other biographical data, although varying in degree of detail, are available reflecting the background, knowledge, experience, judgment, and innate capacity of each of these men. A number of these men have been interviewed to determine their interest in the opening. This personal insight complements the written material.

The position profile details the output expected of the man on the job. It identifies not only the "value added" output that would be regarded as outstanding performance but also the roadblocks and frustrations the man on the job will encounter and must overcome. In addition to this working information, the position profile spells out further working data covering specific responsibilities, authority to act, reporting relationships, performance criteria, and factors effecting organizational "fit." These requirements and expectations are not inflexible. This profile like all tools requires sharpening and reshaping to adjust to change. For the immediate period, however, it puts the position to be filled in the best possible perspective for the purpose at hand.

The third factor that comes into play at this point in setting priorities is the sponsor's credibility. In corralling the names of candidates, men in key spots as well as men in positions corresponding to and closely related to the position to be filled and others who could identify candidates were approached. Advice and suggestions were solicited. Inevitably some of these men proved to be more knowledgeable, discerning, and discriminating than others. Greater weight attaches to the recommendations of these candidates. The men they sponsor should be among the first to be considered.

In establishing priorities for purposes of further consideration of candidates' qualifications, those that head the list should be the men who are already performing at a high level in the functional area under consideration. All that has gone before has been for the purpose of identifying these men.

In zeroing in on these men, the profiles of men recommended by the most credible sponsors should be compared with the position profile for the purpose of making a preliminary assessment of the degree to which men match needs. If what has been done up to this point has been done with the care called for by the nature of the search assignment, there should be a good match between the candidate's profile and the position profile. This is not always found to be true.

A surprise in store for some arises when the profiles of top performers do not match the position profile. When this impasse is encountered, the position profile becomes suspect. It is immediately apparent that the position profile is at variance with the functional structure in other organizations where men are working with a high degree of effectiveness. It is difficult to defend the variant position profiles against the track record of success in other organizations. Valid reasons for exceptions may exist but they result in costly compromises with performance, compromises which candidates will reject. The better practice is to restructure the position profile when it is found to be at variance with established practices proven productive of results.

The degree of match between men and job requirements, added weight having been given a candidate's own track record for achievement along with his sponsor's credibility, establishes priorities for further consideration of candidate qualifications. From this point forward the task is one of assessing the validity of these priorities by probing further into factors which up to this point have been acceptable as prima facie evidence. Presumptions of fact have been presented by sponsors and candidates. Now these presumptions of fact must be probed for the purpose of validating these presumptions. Reversals in priorities may result. The end objective is to identify and place the top performer at the top of the candidate list.

THE RÉSUMÉ: FACT OR FICTION

No man knowingly submits a résumé that presents other than his best face although many men through ignorance or carelessness submit résumés that weaken or destroy their own image of themselves. In the hands of the experienced manager the résumé is a point of departure in researching the record rather than a basis for final judgment of the candidate's capability.

In a search situation referred to earlier, Ken's name headed the priorities for further research. Ken's résumé told Jack, in Ken's words, what Ken had done in the past. Ken had been recommended to Jack by a highly credible source, a man who was familiar with the top performers in Ken's functional area of activity and the area of interest to Jack. Now Jack is commencing to dig deeper to assess Ken's qualifications for the position to be filled.

Jack called Ken and invited him to lunch. During lunch he again told Ken that he was a very promising candidate and added, "Before either of us goes further, with your permission I'd like to talk with a few people who are familiar with your work to make certain that neither of us is overlooking any aspect of this situation that might prove troublesome later. In talking with these people I'll make it clear that I'm interested in learning more about your qualifications. I'll explain that this is not something you have initiated but that I'm asking questions with your permission."

"That's all right with me," Ken said, "talk with anyone outside of the company, but I guess I'd prefer that you not talk inside the house where I work."

"Are there any people in particular that you want to suggest I contact?"

"My former boss would know about my work, of course. Then any of the division heads where I worked before I came here could talk about my work, too. These were the men I provided research recommendations. Giving them good service was my job. As long as I did that I was doing what my boss wanted me to do. I'll give you their names. Talk to any of them. Some of them wanted the impossible and weren't as happy as others but you'll be able to spot pet peeves that will show up."

When candidates are willing to have former associates involved it is usually a sign of strength. It is when a candidate is unwilling to have former associates contacted that their records are suspect. Ken admitted that he hadn't been able to please everyone. At the same time Ken knew that if Jack's judgment was good Jack would spot these men when encountered and if Jack's judgment wasn't good there was little Ken could do about the situation.

From Jack's position men like Ken's former boss and those served earlier by Ken are tactically important contacts. Ken's résumé told Jack things Ken wanted to tell him. Now, Jack is in a position to learn things he wants to know that Ken can't tell him.

No man can see himself as others see him or size himself up as others do. Yet, to a very large degree, these independent judgments have a major impact on all of a man's activities. The strengths and weaknesses which determine much of the effectiveness of what a man does are strengths and weaknesses that are apparent to others. Inherent strengths and weaknesses may not be visible.

It is important to recognize the difference between inherent and apparent strengths and weaknesses. This difference arises in part because weaknesses may hide strengths for some and strengths may hide weaknesses for others. To illustrate, one man may have a thorough understanding of some matter and have a well-thought-out program for action but be unable to sell his ideas to others. A second man may have only a superficial understanding of what's going on and a poor plan of attack but an ability to make his ideas look like panaceas for everyone's problems. Guess whose plan is adopted? An apparent strength hides an inherent weakness in the latter situation while an inherent weakness hides an inherent strength in the former situation.

The man selected to fill an opening enters a situation in which both his apparent capabilities and inherent capabilities become important. His apparent capabilities are his showcase assets. First impressions are important in getting started. In some situations if first impressions aren't favorable, a man never gets a chance to put his inherent capabilities, his functional assets, to work. In researching the record, Jack must audit Ken's apparent capabilities as well as his inherent capabilities.

To do this, at the outset one must avoid asking questions in a way which restricts the response or leads the respondent. Let the man express his thoughts. Don't restrict him or lead him to an answer.

For example, the question, "Do you think Ken could do a good job heading up a marketing research group in a multi-divisional corporation?" is a restrictive and leading question. The respondent must restrict his remarks to his assessment of Ken's capabilities as a head of a marketing research group in a multidivisional corporation. Moreover, the respondent is led to an answer in that he knows Ken must be interested in the position. If he regards Ken as a friend he is led to answer affirmatively; if he doesn't like Ken he will be led toward a negative response.

To audit apparent and inherent capabilities, you ask the question, "We are considering Ken for an opening. Based on your association with Ken what kinds of things does Ken do best?" The respondent is almost sure to ask the nature of the position. When this happens tell him the position will be tailored to capitalize on the successful candidate's capabilities. And that, while you will tell him more about the position before you leave, you would like to hear his assessment of Ken's overall capabilities. Point out that you don't want to overlook any opportunity to capitalize on Ken's full scope of capabilities.

Handled in this manner, the respondent is left no choice other than to talk about the things he believes Ken does best. His observations are in no way restricted and he has no knowledge of comments that are pertinent or immaterial. The respondent's remarks will reflect on a candidate's apparent and inherent capabilities.

A second pertinent question in researching the record is to

ask a reference to comment on activities which the candidate should avoid. No man does each thing equally effectively. A man's associates are usually aware of these weaknesses before the man himself recognizes them. Evidence of weakness does not condemn a candidate if the weaknesses appear in functional areas of lesser importance. More important, in researching the record, is the fact that the reference who can't cite a candidate's weaknesses as well as his strengths probably doesn't know the candidate too well. Anyone who has worked in close association with a man knows his weaknesses as well as his strengths.

A third question to ask Ken's reference is, "If you were to pick a job for Ken that in your opinion would capitalize on his abilities what job would you select?" This can be the most revealing of all answers. It reveals the respondent's thinking about the way in which the candidate can best capitalize on his capabilities and side step his liabilities.

Follow this up by asking, "Why?" This is the clincher. Answers to these four questions not only tell the auditor about the candidate, they tell the auditor about the respondent and whether or not he has been primed by the candidate.

To start with, these questions put the candidate in perspective with respect to his strengths and weaknesses and the way in which these could be applied as well as the rationale supporting this thinking. It forces the reference to think about the candidate's capabilities without a fixed frame of reference other than an earlier association with the candidate.

These questions also put in perspective the man serving as a reference. When you ask a man whether he feels an acquaintance or associate can do a certain job you will get an opinion of one kind or another. Rarely will a man volunteer the information that he doesn't know the individual well enough to reply. You won't learn how well qualified the man is to offer the opinion; you will just get an unqualified answer to your question. Men feel compelled to offer advice.

Ask a man about the things an individual can do best and you will find him reluctant to answer this query unless he knows the individual well. He has been forced to be analytical and evaluative. No longer can he get by with an answer such as, "Sure, so-and-so would be a good man to do such-and-such." Now he must pinpoint things so-and-so does well. He hasn't been given any handle to take hold of; you haven't mentioned any specific function or job. He doesn't want to appear foolish by saying, "So-and-so would make a great salesman" when you may be considering so-and-so for some other job.

Follow this up by asking him about so-and-so's weaknesses and you get an even better bearing on the qualifications of the reference to talk about so-and-so. Weaknesses can be contrasted with strengths. The man whose strength is an ability to move around and meet people, the glad-hander, doesn't usually show up as a man whose weakness is his shy and retiring nature. Such an evaluation of an individual suggests the need for a second look at the things the reference is saying about a man.

Answers to two more questions, "What kind of a position would fully capitalize on so-and-so's capabilities?" and "Why?" tell even more about the ability of the reference to comment on the candidate. Remember, the reference doesn't know the nature of the position for which the candidate is being considered. Without this information he must be objective in thinking about the candidate's capabilities.

The comments made by a qualified reference, that is an observant and articulate respondent who knows the candidate, should present a picture the parts of which fit together. Strengths and weaknesses should not be in conflict. The position which would capitalize on the candidate's strengths should flow logically from suggested strengths and weaknesses and be reflected by the rationale offered in answer to the question, "Why would such-and-such a position best capitalize on so-and-so's capabilities?" When the replies to these questions fit together one can consider that one has been talking to a qualified reference.

However, one word of warning. When all the comments of a respondent tie together so tightly that he homes in too quickly on the position for which the candidate is being considered, the reference has probably been primed by the candidate. Even though they are aware of the position for which a candidate is being considered some men will speak candidly about the candidate while others, thinking they are doing the candidate a favor, will so slant their remarks toward that position that their comments will be of little or no value.

Most candidates aren't so typed for a particular function that a reference will home in on the position for which they are being considered. Van Cliburn's name would be associated immediately with concert performances and the name Menninger is associated with psychiatry, but when one starts by asking questions about strengths and weaknesses, few men fit a single function. When a reference does home in on a specific position right at the outset of his remarks, he is suspect of being less than candid in his comments. Put a big question mark beside such comments when they are recorded in the notes one makes following an interview.

Before closing the interview, ask one more question. Ask the reference to suggest names of individuals who have worked closely or have been closely associated with the candidate on or off the job.

A man who knows a candidate well enough to serve as a reference should certainly know the names of other men who can comment competently on the candidate's qualifications. This is further evidence of his own personal competence to qualify as a reference.

The names suggested may prove to be the same names that were supplied by the candidate. After all, the number of men who are closely associated with anyone in his work is relatively limited. At the same time, the probability is high that additional names will be added that can contribute depth and breadth in researching the candidate's record.

Each man who is acting as a reference should be asked for additional names and these names should be recorded in the notes made following each interview. Whether or not the suggested references are to be interviewed should be determined by the nature of the responses received during previous discussions with other references.

The man experienced in searching for top talent looks for patterns to emerge during discussions with men who know the candidate. He doesn't know what patterns will emerge but he knows that they will emerge. Each man has things he does better than others. He has strengths and he has weaknesses. There are positions for which he is suited and others in which he would be a misfit.

Once behavioral patterns emerge and are verified this part of the process can be brought to a halt. There is no need to do more. The picture is developed. For example, Ken emerged as a man who, among other things, had a well-developed analytical mind and an ability not only to get along well with others but the ability to organize the efforts of others. He was willing to delegate work to others. He introduced new ways of working that multiplied the effectiveness and output of his group.

There were some negatives, too. He did a better job when travel was not required in his work. Ken stayed away from alcohol when he was at home but he drank to excess when he was by himself on trips. This had posed a real problem earlier when he was a salesman and later involved in sales research in the field. Once brought into the office where he could be given closer supervision, he had proved an outstanding performer both in his present position and in his work with his former employer. Because of his ability to produce he had been made a manager of research. In his position he had been an outstanding performer for a number of years.

One other negative was his tendency to let family affairs intrude upon his working day. Either he didn't trust his wife or she didn't trust him, they seemed to be in constant telephone conversation during the day. Literally, he ran the household from the office.

Notwithstanding, he did a job and he wanted recognition for the things he did. He organized the work of his group so that they more than met goals. He knew the things for which brownie points were awarded, and he won the awards. He took pride in performance.

The record has been researched when patterns like this emerge and can be verified. There are other cases in which many different patterns emerge, none of which can be verified. Each attempt to verify the different patterns adds to the complexity of the situation.

The amount of time that can be devoted to researching the record for each of the candidates at the upper end of the list is always limited. The higher the level of the position the greater is the amount of time generally allotted to researching the record. This is shortsighted. The men coming in at the lower levels of the organizational hierarchy are the basic building blocks for the future. When these men are selected with care, subsequent organizational problems are solved before they happen.

The organization that is conducting an all-out search for a president or other corporate officers is the organization that was forced into this position by failure to groom men for the job at lower levels in the hierarchy. Future executives should commence familiarizing themselves with their organizations' activities early in their careers.

4

AUDITING THE ACTION

THE THREE inputs involved in placing the right man on the right job at the right time are position profiles, prospects, and prospect profiles. The output is the right man for the right job at the right time.

But it may be found that additional inputs are needed. The position profile may be poorly defined, too demanding, or reflect a lack of understanding of functional requirements. Prospect profiles may not provide adequate evidence of the prospect's qualifications. Prospects may fail to measure up to needs or so far surpass needs that the man would find no outlet for the full scope of his capabilities. When inputs prove to be unsatisfactory, an earlier part of the process must recycle and return new inputs to the man who must review this documentation and select the man for the job.

Up to this point it would appear that prospects themselves have not played particularly prominent roles. Things are going on around them. They appeared on stage because they were cited as outstanding performers or presented themselves by knocking on the door in response to notice of the opening. Prospects were asked to express their interest, provide biographical data, and suggest references. Since that time, these men have been off the stage in the wings.

There is a sound reason why prospects should be off stage. They did all that there was for them to do. Then it became time for those who could talk about these men and their performance to take their place on the stage. Now the patterns that have emerged from these discussions and data provided earlier by the prospects must be examined in the perspective of position profiles. Following this examination the prospects who look the best will again be brought on stage for the purpose of narrowing the field to a few men or for zeroing in on one man.

In auditing the action three aspects of the record are of primary importance. These three aspects can be approached through three questions.

What does this man want to do? is the first question. During the initial contact, the prospect was asked if he finds that his present assignment gives him ample opportunity to make full use of his talents. His answer to this question is revealing. Ken said that his job didn't always give him ample opportunity to make full use of his talents and added, "I'm impatient. I want to do big things." Ken did not say that he was dissatisfied with what he was doing or that he had other interests he wanted to explore.

The man who has revealed a desire to do more and to enlarge the scope of the things he is doing should receive high marks as a prospect. He wants to move along in the direction in which he is already moving. It is when men want to move in directions that depart from paths in which they have established performance records that they look less attractive as prospects. The position to be filled and for which they might otherwise qualify is not necessarily in line with their interests.

Men do their best job when they are doing things that interest them. Under these circumstances they will put forth extra effort because of the personal pleasure they get from their on-the-job activities. Even though a man has an established record of performance, when he loses interest in the things he has been doing, sooner or later his performance will begin to fall off. The answers men make when asked if present assignments give them an opportunity to make full use of their talents should be audited carefully for telltale signs of shifting interests.

At times men are heard to say such things as, "My job is all right, but I would like to get out of this rat race," "I'd like to have more time to live." or "I like what I'm doing but I would like to do something different for a change." Such comments when made during an earlier interview are candid comments. The man was not necessarily thinking of himself as a prospect. He had been asked to suggest the names of others. As such, these comments are more truly indicative of a man's thinking.

Depending on the situation, comments of this nature may earn a man higher or lower marks. For example, the man who wants to get out of the rat race or wants more time to live might turn out to be the right man for a move to a position in a company located in a smaller town where the pace was slower and commuting not the problem it poses in a metropolitan center. He certainly would not be the man to move to the metropolis.

The man who wants a change in the nature of the action presents a different picture. Most men commenced their careers without giving much thought to the matter. Some took the best paying job they were offered when they left school. Others took a job where their girl friend of the moment lived. Then there were those who went into the family business. Starts like this, while common, represent poor ways for a man to leave the starting gate in running a career course.

At about 40 men begin to take a look at themselves. Up

until then they have been too busy to think about themselves. Marriage, money, and moves to make more money to pay increasing family expenses have filled their thinking time. Then, too, they have been busy with boats, bowling, golf, and grass cutting. They have been too busy to think about what they were doing.

After 15 to 20 years of this, the picture begins to change, as they have time to look at what they are doing and what others are doing. A large number of these men don't like what they see. One man remarked, "I don't even know how I got into the advertising game. All I do all day is to put together some stupid jingles. That's not what I want to do all the rest of my life." This man was "top jingle" in the trade. An art director in the same agency wanted to get out of his management role and into creative work.

Recognition of the need to make a mid-career correction is common among men about the time they reach 40. In one sense it is a good thing. There is still time to make such a correction. In another sense it may be a bad thing. The prospect who is thinking of a mid-career correction that represents a departure from the activity area where he has been an outstanding performer can't expect to carry his performance record with him. For example, the outstanding art director who wants to do creative work may have to start over again at the bottom and prove his ability to do creative work. Men cannot initiate these moves without making sacrifices; they must expect to lose ground in making mid-career corrections.

The man who is thinking in terms of a mid-career correction should be counted out as a prospect in most cases. He represents a liability. He hasn't sorted himself out. It is better to work with a prospect who likes what he is doing but who feels that his present assignment doesn't give him ample opportunity to make full use of his skills. The best prospect knows what he wants. He likes what he is doing. He wants to do more. He wants greater responsibility. He wants it in the functional area in which he has already established a reputation for outstanding performance. About this he has no doubts. He knows what he wants to do.

Is this what you want him to do? then becomes the next question in auditing the action. This question calls for a closer look at the position profile. Earlier, it was pointed out that the controlling question to which the buyer of services should direct his attention was the question, "During the next year, what output from this position would I regard to represent top performance?" The answer to this question more than anything else is prescriptive of the real nature of the function to be performed.

"Value added" expectations define what is wanted. "Value added" is the controlling criterion in thinking about services to be bought by the buyer. Nothing else is more important, but there are other factors that are important parts of the makeup of the position profile drafted as the basis of the search.

No job is without attendant frustrations. Lack of funds and manpower shortages, both in quantity and quality, introduce constraints on action. Policies may introduce additional restraints and rigidity. Possibly the greatest of all frustrations are introduced by the personalities found in every organization. Added to these frustrations are the inevitable conflicts of interest. The man on the job must face up to frustrations.

The position profile also spells out other working data that are prescriptive of the opening to be filled. While value added is the controlling criterion in thinking about performance expectations, there are additional expectations that other duties will be discharged. Responsibilities documented in the position profile are duties thought to be essential to meet the main value added expectation.

A fourth factor relates to authority to act and the limits to this authority. This adds another parameter to the position profile. Both formal and informal reporting relationships affect the future of the man on the job and should be documented.

A fifth factor in the makeup of the position profile relates to performance criteria. These are the finite and relative measures of results achieved. The plan for evaluating the fulfillment of expectations gives definition to performance criteria documents. To the degree that criteria can be expressed in finite numbers to that same degree performance criteria are made more specific but, often, criteria can be expressed only in relative terms.

The final factor, the fit factor, involves such things as environment, custom, temperament, geography, and the social makeup of the situation, what it takes to fit into the situation. There isn't any right or wrong to fit; there is just fit and failure to fit. One can't pick the man who will fit the situation without identifying operative facets of the fit factor.

Time has elapsed since the search commenced. The passing of time is accompanied by change. Before going further, the contents of the position profile should be verified to make certain that the profile accurately portrays the position to be filled. When position profiles are audited surprising things surface.

The job may no longer exist. In one case a search was conducted for a man to develop a conveyor system for a manufacturing plant that was part of a multidivisional corporation. The man wanted was familiar with ways of automating manufacturing operations. The objective was to eliminate manual labor and to make possible rapid changeover from model to model. An audit of the position profile after prospects had been contacted and prior to further screening of prospects revealed that the plant had been sold, but no one had informed the man responsible for recruiting personnel.

More frequently, changes in management thinking evolve. In one company while a search was under way for a corporate director of commercial development who would report to the president, the president left to join another company. The man who replaced him had quite different ideas about what he expected a director of corporate development to do on the job. Moreover, the former president believed that men performed best when allowed freedom to set their own working hours. The new president used binoculars to survey the executive parking lot each morning to check on late arrivals. Not only had the position to be filled changed in makeup but the environment in which the new man would work had changed, too.

Once an audit verifies the accuracy of a position profile, changes having been made where necessary, you are in a position to compare the pattern of action a prospect wants to engage in with the pattern of action presented by the position profile. The closer the fit, the greater the assurance that the candidate will continue to perform in the position. The greater the gap between the two patterns, the greater the uncertainty of a carry-over of capabilities and a projection of past performance into the future in the event the prospect is selected to fill the opening.

The best prospect is looking for an opportunity to make better use of his skills by moving to a position of greater responsibility in a functional area in which he has already established an ability to perform. This is why in auditing the action it is important to verify and compare both what the prospect wants to do and what is wanted by the buyer of services.

Is he qualified to do this? is the third question to ask in auditing the action. Priorities among prospects placed some men at the top of the list and others lower on the list. When an audit has verified a high degree of compatibility between what a man wants to do and what the buyer of services wants done, it is time to audit the prospect's qualifications for performance.

The best evidence of a man's qualification to do a job is the fact that he has done the job and done it well. There isn't any better evidence. The auditor's job is to test the validity and credibility of the evidence. Evidence is not proof. Evidence of performance is not proof of performance; it substantiates performance. When someone says, "Don does an outstanding job," the auditor is offered evidence. Having been offered evidence, in auditing the action the auditor tests the evidence. Evidence that passes the test becomes acceptable as proof of performance.

At the outset of the audit the auditor sweeps aside the snowflakes, looks for stated accomplishments and arranges these in chronological order in his thinking placing the prospect's most recent achievements at the top of the audit schedule. Sometimes the evidence is swept away with the snowflakes because there was no solid evidence to examine.

For example, Don headed the list in a search for a manager of new product development. Reference after reference had pointed to Don's record of a new product a year during the three years he had been on the job. Each product was a high profit producer.

Don had joined the company three years previously. Well liked by everyone, he was a popular speaker and a dedicated missionary for new product development. New product development was the subject of many published papers authored by Don.

An audit of Don's interests had established beyond doubt Don's interest in enlarging the scope of his activities. Don's interests matched the position profile. The auditor's job was to test the validity and credibility of the evidence. The evidence offered was Don's popularity as a speaker and writer as well as a record of three product winners in three years. The position profile told the auditor that the creation of product winners was what the buyer of services wanted, not published papers and talks, so attention was focused on the product winners. Questions in the auditor's mind were: Did Don initiate the products? and were they winners? Auditors are professional doubters; that is their job.

This evidence was in line with what was wanted by the buyer of services. The evidence remaining after the snow-flakes, published papers, and talks had been swept away passed the first test; it was relevant. The next test was to establish the validity of the evidence. Did Don, in fact, produce three new products as alleged?

To learn more about this the auditor talked with the company's Manager of Research and Engineering about the company's new product activities. During this discussion the auditor learned some interesting things. All three products had been in the works for a year or so before Don joined the company. The ideas had been generated by the marketing manager who had good market sensitivity. As the Manager of R and E put it, "Rick, our marketing manager, can spot a profitable idea a mile away." Market research and technical feasibility studies had substantiated Rick's belief that the products would be winners and the ideas were put into the works.

Don came along about the time that the prototypes were ready. While Don had done extensive promotion of the products, he had not contributed any ideas for new products to follow the three just introduced. This concerned the R and E manager because he had expected the new product program to accelerate rather than decelerate when Don took over as new product manager. This position was established to supplement and augment the flow of ideas from other sources.

Again, expressing an interest in the way the company developed new products, the auditor talked with the marketing manager and another man who headed up marketing research. Both men substantiated the fact that Don was a great promoter, hinting that he promoted Don more than products, but that Don had not contributed a single idea for a new product during his three years with the company. It was also apparent that this was coming to the notice of top management.

The audit trail now led to Don's former employer. Here, too, the auditor learned that Don's success with new product's was traceable to his inheritance, products that were already in the works when Don first arrived. Don had added nothing new in the pipeline. Don left when this became apparent. Don's successor had the job of developing a crash program to get new products under way again.

The auditor had arrived at the end of the audit trail. New evidence replaced old evidence and the new evidence had been validated to the satisfaction of the auditor. Don was a personality but not a performer. Don knew this, was clever enough to trade on this, and managed the timing so that he moved in on a job where he could survive for a period on his predecessor's performance. Those who recommended Don were sincere in thinking that Don was a performer because he was a charmer. It was an old story, one the auditor had heard before. It was the reason for auditing the action.

It can't be emphasized too often that the best evidence of a man's ability to perform on a job is the fact that he has done the job and done it well. There isn't any better evidence, but evidence isn't proof of performance. It substantiates performance. Proof of performance results from testing the validity and credibility of evidence. This is the reason for auditing the action.

Often men are able to explain away their failures by attributing them to circumstances beyond their control. On the wheel of fortune, the numbers fall both ways. The laws of probability so dictate. Just as men's failures are fortunes of war, men's successes, too, are fortunes of war. Successes may be due to circumstances beyond their control. The auditor must be judge and jury.

Other things may be learned during the audit, too. For

example, Rick's name had not appeared on the prospect list. Rick was the marketing manager in the company where Don worked. The manager of R and E had commented that Rick could spot a profitable idea a mile away. The auditor sensed that a man like Rick was needed for the job. He added Rick's name high up on the prospect list with a resulting realignment of prospect priorities.

Auditing the record almost always results in a realignment of prospect priorities. Some names like Don's are dropped. New names, as in the case of Rick, may be added. The process of zeroing in on the man for the job is well along at this point. The next step audits the man himself.

AUDITING THE MAN

The prospect who left the stage earlier now returns from the wings, that is, if he is one of the top two or three on the list. It may be that none of the prospects survived the audit of the record. When this unfortunate situation occurs, the search must begin again, because something went wrong.

The prospects to whom attention is now directed are regarded as the finalists. Much time and attention have already been given them. Their interest in the position has been verified. Their pattern of activities matches that of the opening, and their ability to perform has been validated. There is no doubt that anyone of these finalists can measure up as a performer, but value added expectations can be met on the job only when the man can overcome frustrations, accept responsibility, act within defined areas of authority, and fit an organization's makeup.

A preliminary review of the record gave the prospects good marks in these respects, but a closer look is necessary when men become finalists. There is a difference between the man who can do the job and the man who can work effectively within a particular organizational setting. Initially, the thrust in the search was directed at identifying top performers. Now the thrust shifts to determining which of these men can do the job best.

Factors other than value added were not overlooked earlier. However, there is a limit to the time and attention that can be given to each prospect in the early phases of a search. Moreover, once top producers are identified and validated, the probability is good that these men will measure up in other respects, too. After all, they have already performed well in other situations.

Finding the man for the job is commonly called recruiting, but there is a better name for this function, one that focuses attention on the aspect of the search that determines the difference between finding a man and finding the best man. The term, of course, is auditing. Recruitment is largely an auditing function, a matter of verifying the validity and credibility of evidence submitted to support an allegation of an ability to perform.

As in auditing the written record, there is a need to audit the finalists, themselves. It is time to go back to the top two or three finalists and tell each of them (after giving more thought to an earlier talk or a review of a résumé that has been submitted) it appears that it would be worthwhile to talk further about the position. Finalists have had time to think more about the matter, and they should be asked if they are still interested in exploring the subject.

Earlier, each of these men indicated some interest in the position. However, a man's thinking may have changed. If so, it is better to concentrate on the finalists who still want to explore the opening. The man who wants to think about a move, the open-minded man, is the better prospect. The man who really wants to make better use of his talents and achieve more in his specialty is willing to talk and perform should the position prove an opportunity for achieving his goals.

In his conversations with each of these finalists, the auditor's primary concern is with the way in which the man would fit into the organization. Some men will fit in almost anywhere; others who work effectively in one situation could not work well in other situations. In drafting the position profile, certain characteristics were grouped together as fit factors, but at this point reporting relationships, authority, and performance criteria also come into play as determinants of the effectiveness with which a man can work in a new situation.

The top performer in a small company, for example, may not be able to work effectively in a larger organization. Townsend, a top performer as sales manager in a smaller company was a finalist in one search. When it came time to talk with him in greater detail about the position for which he was being considered, Townsend learned that in the larger organization marketing research reported to a manager of marketing research who was on the same organizational level as the sales manager. Moreover, sales service reported to a manager of customer relations. While Townsend as sales manager in the new situation would have three times the number of people in his own part of the organization, he did not feel that he could do a job unless he had control of marketing research and sales service.

Mark, as manager of administrative services in one company, had authority to add to his staff as needed and to terminate unsatisfactory performers. While the position under consideration offered him a greater opportunity to exercise his skills, staffing was controlled by personnel services. Mark would not accept a position which placed limits on his authority to hire and fire.

In another situation, Ned would not consider a manufacturing assignment in which his salary would be based in part on his realization of production quotas, time schedules, and quality ratings. He said that he was willing to do the best he could, and it appeared that he would be an outstanding man for the job, but he didn't want to be graded at the end of each day.

Auditing finalists places two demands on the auditor. He

must have intimate knowledge of the situation in which the man works and will work, and he must be able to size up men. The man who has been a dictator doesn't fit into an organization that functions as a democracy, and the democrat going in as the manager of a group that has been run as a dictatorship is in trouble. The man who has been accustomed to setting his own working hours as needed to do the job doesn't always adjust to an eight-to-five routine enforced for all of the brass. The auditor must size up the man and the situation to determine which man would best fit the existing situation. While he might like to hope that either the one factor or both would change to accommodate the other, action on such an assumption is overly optimistic and imprudent.

The auditor has every opportunity to learn about the situation surrounding the opening for which he is searching for the right candidate. The personalities involved are present and available for his examination and assessment. The only explanation for failure to size up this situation is lack of due diligence on the part of the auditor. This is not true with respect to the prospects and the situations in which they are found. Here the personalities involved are present but not necessarily available for examination and assessment. This examination and assessment must be made by talking with the prospect himself. There is no one best way of doing this, but some guidelines can prove helpful.

When the prospect affirms his continued interest in the position, tell him that the biographical data he supplied were useful in bringing the discussion to the present stage. Thus this substantiated, along with the comments of his references his qualifications. Point out that it is always necessary to sell others in the organization on a prospective candidate's capabilities. For this purpose it would be helpful to have pertinent and timely data in greater detail. Ask him to talk about some of his most recent achievements.

As the prospect talks about these things, he should be interrupted occasionally and asked whether or not he faced any resistance or frustrations in the course of attaining his objectives. As he talks about these obstacles, the auditor should reflect on the probability that these same frustrations or similar frustrations may exist in the position under consideration. The man who has effectively overcome these problems in the past can be expected to overcome them in the future. The man who has not overcome frustrations in the past should not be expected to overcome them in the future.

In discussing his frustrations a prospect will almost always introduce personalities into the picture. For example, one man's complaint was the fact that he was expected to act on his own initiative too much of the time. While he enjoyed the freedom and took advantage of the opportunity to do the things he thought should be done, he felt, as he expressed it, "as if I am flying blind too much of the time." The auditor recognized that this man would be faced with the same problem on the new job. Since the man seemed to know how to control the situation successfully, the auditor merely complimented him on his ability to act on his own and explained that in the position under consideration he would also be expected to "fly blind."

It is also good practice to ask a man to talk about the things he knows are his weaknesses. The man who is aware of his ability to perform knows he has weaknesses, and he capitalizes on this knowledge by avoiding situations which would play on his weaknesses rather than his strengths. Moreover, top performers concentrate their time and attention on the development of their strengths rather than their weaknesses. The man who doesn't recognize his weaknesses doesn't know how to stay out of trouble, nor does he know how to apply his personal development time in a manner which will yield him the greatest returns. The man who talks candidly and articulately about his weaknesses reveals an important strength: the ability to avoid his weaknesses, the ability to avoid the action areas that spell trouble for him.

Another aspect of a man's thinking that is important to the

auditor is the matter of his thoughts and plans for the future. The man who has plans for the future that are a logical projection of his capabilities has sorted himself out. The man who stumbles around with the answer to this question is not a man who can take command and provide direction in a new situation.

The answer to this question reveals other important information. It provides the auditor an opportunity to assess the compatibility of a prospect's plans with the aims and goals of the functional area represented by the position under consideration. Two questions are particularly pertinent. Are his plans ambitious enough to satisfy the needs of the new assignment? And are his plans too ambitious to be digested by management?

The man who says he wants to walk on the moon or one of the planets has ambitious plans. His plans qualify him as a prospect for the flight crew at NASA's Manned Spacecraft Center but they are too ambitious to be digested by flight crew managers of a commercial airline. The lawyer who wants to develop a corporate legal group with top flight anti-trust expertise also has plans that cannot be digested by a small company that needs a man to manage contracts, conveyances, and labor relations. The engineer who wants to create new products won't fit in with a group dedicated to the preservation of established product lines.

The man whose plans and programs fall short of management's thoughts about the future is a poor prospect for a new assignment in an organization that has plans for growth. In particular, one must be on the watch for the man whose plans suggest that he has a reluctance to relocate. Many men resist moving their households and limit their plans for the future to activities and projects that don't necessitate moves. When this happens, the man on the job can impede corporate growth until this action is detected and corrected.

Watch out for the top performer who is topping off or leveling out on a plateau. There is a tendency on the part of some men to reach a level in their progress when they become content to sit back and take it easy. The real danger results from the assumption that one can rest on one's past reputation and continue to do things as they have always been done. Unfortunately for these men, they are operating in a dynamic milieu. Change is taking place constantly. Those who are through growing are, indeed, through.

A man's plans for the future are a good indicator of whether or not he is "through." His plans for the future should make it clear that he is not topping off at his present level of activity, and these plans should be compatible with the thinking of management. They should be ambitious enough to meet the needs of the opening but not so ambitious that the man's plans would prove indigestible.

Another question that returns good yield on time spent in auditing a man is this: "What aspects of the position for which you are being considered have the greatest appeal?" The men who stress such things as the opportunity to enlarge the scope of their activities and to take on added responsibilities prove to be the best prospects for positions where high level achievement is expected. Prospects who stress such things as security and fringe benefits are the men who reveal symptoms suggesting that they are getting ready to sit back and watch the world go by.

Along with this same question, a man should be asked to express his thoughts about the "negatives" he sees in the situation. He may see things that should be changed. He's been a top performer, experienced in the functional area. In most cases the best prospects know more about the job than the man they are talking to about the position. Their experience is firsthand. The auditor's experience is secondhand.

The prospect who makes constructive suggestions provides further evidence of his ability to grow on the job. One man being considered for a position as manager of a company's management information systems group said that the aspect of the position that had least appeal to him was the fact that the present computer configuration was too large for the company's needs. It would be difficult to justify. At the same time he sensed that it was the pride and joy of one of the vice presidents who had been responsible for the installation. In view of this, he didn't look forward to the job of rescaling the hardware to fit needs.

Constructive criticism reveals men's insight and analytical ability. Things can be done better ways, and these men are aware of this. When men who respond to a query about negatives comment on things that can't be changed, this kind of criticism suggests that the man may not adjust to certain constants in the situation. Situational constants include location of the place where the job will be performed, a need to travel to perform effectively on certain assignments, size of company, and product identification or image. These things change slowly. When men cite these things as negative aspects of a situation, such comments raise warning signals in the mind of the experienced auditor.

A final question you should ask a man is what things he is doing to further his personal development? A man's earlier educational preparation is not particularly pertinent. This was his ticket that provided him his early interviews. Since then he trades on his on-the-job acquired knowledge and experience.

This does not mean that his earlier educational experience was of no value; it means that the value of this earlier education is reflected in his achievements. He has proved to himself the value of formal education by his accomplishments. It is of no concern that the man went to a certain school and took a particular course. What really matters is what a man took away with him that he put to use. His record of achievement tells this story.

A man's present personal development program is a different matter. The engineer who finds he needs to know more about accounting or law or the lawyer who needs to know engineering may be taking evening study courses. The man who is doing something significant to further his own personal development looms larger as an attractive prospect than the man who is doing nothing to further his personal development.

THE FINAL SUMMATION

Finally, the auditor must spread out his notes, sit back, review them, and come to a conclusion about the man for the job. The evidence has been collected and its validity tested. If it doesn't reveal the man for the job, the cycle must start over again.

One thing must be remembered. At best, the evidence is circumstantial. No one can ever be sure that the man selected is, in fact, the best man for the job. The final choice is a considered judgment.

The better the knowledge of the man's performance the better the chances are for a valid judgment. The performance record of men who have been with a company for a period of years provides a better basis for judgment than the record of relative "strangers." More is known about the company man. The credibility and validity of available evidence is greater. The man within the company who looks 75 to 100 percent as good as a prospect from outside proves, in most cases, to be the better choice.

In the final summation there is no formula that can be applied. The choice of the man for the job must be a matter of judgment based on the credibility and validity of available evidence.

5

AVOIDING THE PITFALLS

In SEARCHING, screening, and selecting men, the following mistakes have proved pitfalls in the past.

1. Attempts have been made to fit the misfit.
2. Efficiency has been confused with effectiveness.
3. Weaknesses have been expected to disappear.
4. Turnabouts in performance have been anticipated.
5. Number two men have been selected over number one men.
6. Selection has been made by eliminating negatives.
7. Decisions have been made while doubts existed.

These same mistakes will be made in the future unless those responsible for searching, screening, and selecting men familiarize themselves with these pitfalls. All managers can learn from experience; effective managers save time when they learn from the experience of others. Valuable lessons can be learned from W. J.

Listen to W. J. as he tells his personnel manager why he has selected Bill for an important assignment.

"I've looked over the candidates and decided to give Bill the job of salesman in the Southwest territory. This is an important spot because the man who goes into the area will replace Tom when he retires at the end of the year. This is my thinking in selecting Bill.

"Bill is a hard-sell man and, while our sales policies and programs are pitched around a soft sell, his sales record measures up to our average per salesman. Bill doesn't know our product line or the territory, but tests showed that Bill can read twice as fast as any of our salesmen as a result of the time and attention he has given to speed reading. He will be a fast learner because, with his fast reading, he can winnow the wheat from the chaff. Several of his references pointed out that he has a record of occasional lost days due to a tendency toward alcoholism, but he promises to correct this at once. Also, while he has been a loner, in our group he'll soon catch the team spirit. Then, too, he's the Number Two man for our competitor's field manager and that, alone, tells us he's prime material. His title is salesman but as Number Two in his territory I see him as a field manager already although he admits he has a bad record when it comes to customer sales reports and, as he puts it, the unnecessary detail work. One reference even said that Bill didn't bother to read new product releases or, for that matter, mail from the head office. That comment doesn't make sense to me. Bill took a speed-reading course and look at the test scores.

"I arrived at Bill's name after going down the list of prospects. Joe doesn't know our product line. Al lacks experience and Pete is priced too high for our blood. While I'm not so sure how our customers will react to Bill, I'm aware he is a loudmouth, I've decided to give him a chance at the job even though I have a lot of doubts about his ability to make the grade."

Sound familiar? It should. It reflects the manner in which many men are picked. W. J. has made all seven mistakes managers make in picking the man for the job. Want to avoid them? The best way to do this is to study W. J.'s mistakes so that it won't be necessary to repeat them. In other words, learn from the experience of others.

ATTEMPTING TO FIT THE MISFIT

Men who were equally outstanding performers in two different organizations have proved to be poor performers in a third organization. Why? Because the way they did things was incompatible with the way in which things were done in a third organization. The men didn't fit the new picture.

The organizational working style is the sum total of individual working styles. Bring men together and individual styles become the organizational style. This comes about in different ways.

Men tend to join organizations that have a working style that pleases them personally. The aggressive salesman joins a high powered selling group that places high rewards on performance. The scientific authority joins a group where he will have freedom to pursue his interests. The man who feels insecure joins an organization with highly structured rules of conduct and practice. The hometown boy joins a group made up of hometown boys.

In other words, organization styles are developed and strengthened as like attracts like. But how do organizational styles originate? In part, a group's function determines style. Auditing teams, for example, follow prescribed procedures that impose conformity on members.

Superimposed on all of this, leaders evolve and leaders impose rules. In one organization, dark suits, white shirts, conservative ties, and wing-tipped shoes are the order of the day. In another organization, this attire identifies one as behind the times. In one organization, executives leave at the end of the day with bulging briefcases full of homework. In another organization, this suggests incompetence and inability to act effectively. In one organization, decisions are handed down. In another organization, men are expected to make their own decisions. One organization acts through committees; another organization has a policy prohibiting the formation of committees.

Who is right and who is wrong? In the situations cited everyone is right. Those at each extreme cited have been successful. Performance has been high. However, in each situation, there have been dropouts. The dropouts moved to other situations where they became successes. Why? Because they moved to groups having different working styles, working styles compatible with their own individual styles.

Everyone is aware that a square peg will not fit a round hole. Nor will a round peg fit a square hole. Yet, repeatedly, men are selected for positions in groups in which the prevailing working style is not compatible with individual working styles. When this happens, men prove to be misfits, and the experience proves costly in terms of time and money to all concerned.

The human dynamo, driver, and ball-roller will not fit into the slow-moving group. The sell-and-run salesman won't fit a sell-and-serve organization. The committeeman worker won't fit the loose-knit group of entrepreneurs in which every man is expected to make it on his own. The autocrat won't fit into a group in which action is expected only after in-depth analysis, checking, double checking, and consultation with superiors, peers, and subordinates.

Misfits are mismatched. One group's misfit may be another group's star performer. Almost every top performer can cite one or more situations in which he was a dropout because he didn't fit the working style of a particular group.

While some men are highly flexible and adaptable, top performers have usually developed a comfortable working style, which is one of their sources of success. Expectations of a compromise with this working style should be accompanied by expectations of a compromise with performance. The general rule applicable is: Don't attempt to fit the misfit. Be sure the prospect fits into the group.

An exception is the situation in which an individual is selected for the purpose of changing the working style of the group. This is a different ball game. Now the incumbents on the job are declared misfits by executive fiat. The group's style is to be shaken into a new working style. Round holes are to be made square or square holes round. The new man's working style is to become the new working style. The group's style is to fit the candidate's style. Under such circumstances, a waiver of the general rule, "Don't attempt to fit the misfit," is in order.

MISTAKING EFFICIENCY FOR EFFECTIVENESS

A man's obviously apparent efficiency on an assignment often obscures his real effectiveness on the job. For example, Art is a clean desk man who works from his in-basket to his out-basket taking things in order, from top to bottom, as they arrive on his desk. He has taken a speed-reading course and is the only man in his office who is able to read everything that crosses his desk. Moreover, at the end of the day, armed with a portable Dictaphone, Art takes all that is left over home with him to complete so that he is ready to start the next day with a clean desk.

Art eliminated the lunch hour. "Too time consuming," he says, "I eat a sandwich at my desk and add an hour to my working day, or two and a half hours the way some of my associates drag out a lunch hour." To further increase his efficiency, Art makes use of a Speakerphone so that he can work with his hands and talk on the telephone at the same time. "Why do just one job when you can do two?" asks Art. One never even talks with Art when he isn't shuffling some papers on his desk.

Art is always looking for better ways of doing what he is doing. "Study the job," advises Art, "it's the only way to discover how to do things in the shortest time." When a working philosophy of this kind is put into practice, men discover that efficiency has a good track record for getting them where they don't want to be when they arrive, because they didn't give any thought to the "why" of what they were doing.

To return to an earlier statement, a man's efficiency on an assignment often obscures his effectiveness on the assignment. Art is not to be criticized for his efficiency but for his failure to be effective. If efficiency does not produce the desired results, how effective is his action?

Improving the means to achieve desired ends is worthwhile only when the ends themselves are worthwhile. The efficient man focuses all of his time and energy improving means at the expense of ends. The effective man is concerned, first, with the worthwhileness of what is being done or is to be done. The efficient man often finds that he has worked out the best way of doing something that wasn't worth doing.

Effective action starts with the identification and assessment of the worthwhileness of the end results to be achieved. One can't act effectively pounding sand in the proverbial rat hole but one can be efficient. Action can't be effective when the end results aren't worthwhile.

The pitfall to be avoided in picking the man for the job is that efficiency is much more readily apparent than effectiveness. One can always spot the man, for example, who puts his time to work doing two things while another man does one. It is more difficult to determine whether the two things the first man is doing are as important as the one thing the second man is doing. The world is full of hard workers who are accomplishing less than others who are expending less effort but doing more worthwhile things.

Not only does efficiency obscure effectiveness but busyness is often confused with efficiency. An assumption is made that the man on the run knows where he is going, an assumption that usually proves to be false. The man moving unobtrusively, not running, is probably the one who knows where he is going. He selected his destination, planned his trip, and started on time. Why run?

It is amusing to observe the men in airport club lounges who are continually on the run, making telephone calls while waiting for flights. They appear to be men who make every minute count—but is this the case? Listen to their conversation; you can't help hear them talk. Their calls fall into a familiar pattern of nuisance calls. They are calls to tell acquaintances they are at the airport waiting for a flight. Who cares? These are "busyness" calls not business calls. Without seeming to be aware of it, these men are making nuisance calls. The contacts they think they are making are contacts they are terminating. Effective men don't want their time taken up by a "busynessman."

The busy man's performance and the efficient man's performance must be measured on the basis of results not on the basis of busyness or efficiency. Results are what count. Effective men don't attract attention by either busyness or efficiency; rather, they attract attention as producers of results.

The effective man studies the situation not the job. He is interested in the What? Why? Where? Who? and When? questions before he becomes involved in the How? questions. He knows that it is what you do that counts not how you do it. How you do it is ancillary. He knows that doing something better isn't worthwhile if that something isn't worthwhile. The effective man knows that it isn't the means but the ends that count. He doesn't get mired in technique and technology. He is not a technician, but a selector of direction. He is the man who concerns himself with where he is going, first, before he gets involved in the mechanics of travel.

The general applicable rule is: "Don't mistake efficiency for effectiveness. Look at end results rather than means to the ends. Pick the man who is producing the worthwhile results. It takes more skill and time to assess a man's ability to act effectively than his ability to act efficiently. However, it is worth the effort. Who wants men around who can't distinguish between worthwhile things to do and things that aren't worth doing?

Again, there is an exception to the general rule. Those who want to call the shots themselves, who don't want men thinking about the end results of their efforts, who want men to concentrate their attention on the means to ends, who want slave labor, should select efficient men not the effective men. Under these circumstances, pick the efficient man. The effective man won't work in a slave labor camp.

EXPECTING WEAKNESSES TO DISAPPEAR

Everyone has strengths and weaknesses. The wise man is aware of his strengths and weaknesses, admits their existence, and attempts to work around them. That is, the wise man capitalizes on his strengths and avoids situations in which weaknesses will create problems for him and others.

When being considered for new positions, men become acutely conscious of their personal weaknesses. When this happens, men are prompted to make promises to correct weaknesses, promises rarely fulfilled. A weakness a man hasn't corrected in the past can't be expected to be corrected in the future. He has had time in the past to correct weaknesses and passed up opportunities, as he will in the future.

In picking the man for the job, your best candidate is the man whose strengths are those needed by the assignment on which he is placed. Selection should be based on these strengths. These strengths should offset weaknesses which should not be expected to go away. Why should they suddenly disappear? There is no reason why well-developed weaknesses should go away because a man is on a new assignment. Along with his strengths, a man should be expected to bring his weaknesses to the new job.

The point to be made is to hire on strengths without expecting weaknesses to be corrected. For example, one alcoholic is a marketing genius. It might be hoped that he will correct his drinking problem. There are few who surpass him in marketing acumen and skills. Those who wish to take advantage of his talents should expect this weakness to accompany him to the new assignment; it has always accompanied him to new assignments in the past as it will in the future.

The general appplicable rule is: Don't expect weaknesses to disappear; hire for strengths. To this rule there is no waiver. While this may present a pessimistic point of view, the experience of the past suggests that the realistic picture is just that, pessimistic, when assessing the probability that weaknesses will be corrected.

All of this begs the question, can't men be expected to change or develop with the passing of time? Yes, they can and do but not while making adjustments to new assignments and working environments. Don't gamble on candidates whose strengths don't offset their weaknesses. Select the candidate whose strengths offset his weaknesses and don't expect his weaknesses to disappear.

ANTICIPATING TURNABOUTS

There is nothing in the record of the experience of the past to suggest that the salesman who is the top producer in the territory will be effective as a district manager. There is nothing in recorded experience to suggest that an outstanding research scientist will be a good director of research. The politician proves to be devious but not effective on administrative assignments.

Why? The answer: Present patterns of performance reflect

past patterns rather than anticipated patterns. Patterns of performance change slowly if at all.

The highly creative man, the man who takes pride in the things he does, the tireless worker who wants to be his own boss, set his own hours, work on the things he wants to work on, and is highly productive, for example, doesn't turn about and make a good manager of creative people. Placed in a management position, he continues to act as a loner and to let others manage themselves.

The operating manager who is an outstanding producer working in a daily crossfire of problems, performing under the pressure of deadlines in an office crowded by associates demanding answers to questions, with telephones ringing constantly, proves to be a poor man for the long-range planning position where he is to be called upon to work in relative isolation thinking about tomorrow, not today.

Men often present themselves as candidates for positions demanding patterns of performance different from those demanded of them in the past because of an expressed change in personal interests. Some of these changes of interest are genuine. More often they are motivated by such things as a desire to earn more money, to dodge an unwanted job, or to keep one step ahead of the firing line. Regardless of the reason, a man's interest in a job offers poor assurance of his ability to perform in a situation demanding a different pattern of performance than his past pattern of performance. This is one of the reasons why so many politically appointed public office holders are do-nothing men. There is no reason to expect them to be able to perform in a pattern differing from that of the ward wheeler-dealer.

A man's performance pattern develops slowly. It is a composite of his background, knowledge, skills, experience, and innate capacity. With the passing of time interests, opportunities, and options change. These changes have an impact on his pattern of performance but take place slowly without dramatic suddenness.

A man's professed interest in an activity which is not compatible with a projection of his past pattern of performance should not be permitted to overshadow the fact that a man's expressed interest does not offer a scintilla of evidence of his ability to perform. Many men are willing literally, to try anything. They are intrigued by challenge and change.

Interest, willingness, and effort are weak words compared with performance, productivity, and results. In picking the man for the job, you are buying services. You should buy proved performance. This does not mean that once a man's performance is cast in a mold the pattern cannot be changed. It can be changed, but it takes time and effort. He must determine the changes he wants to make. Then, he must sieze opportunities to make these changes. They must be made slowly in a way which will permit him to establish new and salable patterns of performance while pursuing activities at performance levels which are salable. Attempts to move to new activity areas by job jumping end in disaster when men find that they are unable to compete with more effective producers.

Buyers of services should give careful consideration to the man who developed a new and salable pattern of performance as part of a planned program. He will have done this while he was selling his already salable services. There are always opportunities to slowly shift the emphasis of things one is doing, to try one's skill at new activities, and to take evening courses to develop one's competence in new areas of interest. This is the only way in which men can change established patterns of performance and offer new patterns of knowledge, experience, and skills worthy of the consideration of buyers of services.

The general applicable rule is: Don't anticipate turnabouts, expect projections of the past. Those who have violated this rule either through ignorance or thinking that a man's interest in change and willingness to accept challenge, learn from their own experience what they could have learned from the experience of others. They learn that they can only pick the top performers on the basis of projections of past performance and not on optimistically anticipated turnabouts. This is one rule you cannot waive.

SEARCHING FOR NUMBER TWO

In initiating a search for a man, executives are frequently heard to say, "What I'm looking for is the number two man." For example, an executive may need a manufacturing manager and set out to locate a manufacturing manager's number two man to fill a number one man spot. In other instances searches are initiated to locate the number two men in a controller's department, insurance department, research and development group, and so on, and again, to fill a number one man spot.

The idea that a number two man exists is a snare and delusion that should be laid to rest as quickly as possible. Executives searching for number two men labor under the belief that lurking relatively unnoticed somewhere in some organizations are second in command men who are as capable as the first in command men and who really carry the load and do the work. Reasoning further along these same lines these executives feel that if you search out the number two men and put them in charge you will have a real winner.

The experience of the past suggests that one is more likely to end up a loser along with the number two man himself. There may be some top talent hidden in the number two spot in some organizations but, for the most part, the number two man is the number two man for good reason. The number two man may be inexperienced, lack initiative and leadership, or be unwilling to accept responsibility. For that same reason he can't perform as number one elsewhere. He hasn't developed, as yet, to the degree necessary to move up either in his own organization or any other organization.

Whatever the reason, why gamble? Is it worth the risk when it may prove necessary to move several number two level men in and out of a job to find the right man for the job? The better course to follow is to search for a number one man for the number one spot. Seach and select the man with a proven record of performance in the position in which he is to be placed.

The general applicable rule is: Don't look for number two; look for number one. An exception to all of this arises when a thorough search by a competent team fails to turn up the right candidate. Now, the situation is different. It may be necessary to turn one's sights toward the number two man.

Under these circumstances, the position profile should be reviewed in recognition of the fact that it is to be filled by a compromise candidate. Some restructuring of reporting relationships and the assignment itself may be in order, a shifting of authority and responsibilities to tailor the assignment to the best available candidate. These changes in the profile should be in effect until such time as the man selected establishes his ability to assume the full duties of the assignment. Remember, he has not functioned as a number one man; he has been a number two man.

Moreover, additional time should be set aside to work with him to help him orient himself to the situation and organization. Note that reference is made to additional time. The word additional is added because time should be set aside to help any new man on an assignment orient himself to the unfamiliar situation and organization. Too often, a man is left to find his own way around and, while a good man will do this, he will waste less time and have greater success, which means he will make fewer mistakes, when he is guided by men who should know the right route to follow. In this respect the number two man is no different from the number one man, except for the fact that being less experienced he will need more help and guidance.

SELECTING BY ELIMINATING NEGATIVES

The man picked for the job is the candidate who was left on the list after other names were crossed off the list for the wrong reasons. The best candidate is often eliminated early in the screening process.

In filling a position, one executive reviewed a group of résumés received in response to an advertisement in the *Wall Street Journal*. As a first step, he eliminated all of those who did not have a college degree from a four-year college. Then after taking a look at what was left he went through the remaining résumés and eliminated those over forty years of age. Next, he interviewed candidates and dropped from further consideration candidates he considered to be overweight, too talkative, or who appeared to have made too many moves in recent years. The remaining candidate was offered the job.

Within a year it was apparent that the new man had neither the job knowledge needed to make sound decisions nor the necessary management ability. In the meantime a competitor had hired one of the rejected candidates for the position and the competitor was moving to a leadership position in the industry as a result of this man's contributions.

Managers who pick men by eliminating negatives focus their thinking in the wrong direction. It isn't what you don't want that is important, it is what you do want that is important in filling a position. However, it is always easier for managers to be specific about things that they don't want than to be specific about things that they do want. Through force of habit negatives loom large in the thinking of many managers.

First and foremost, a manager should be looking for a candidate who can do what has to be done. This calls for a current, comprehensive, and specific statement of immediate and longer range functions involved in the assignment. This is the controlling document for the search. Nothing should be "hung on" to this document that isn't part of the functional requirement of the assignment.

For example, if a man is needed to head up a team to develop and introduce a new product in the farm equipment field a search should be undertaken for a man who knows farm equipment, a man who has been involved in both the development and introduction of new farm equipment, and a man who has had project management experience.

Should the search turn up a number of candidates, these candidates should be ranked, first, on the basis of breadth of experience in new product development, marketing, and management. Second, candidates should be ranked on the basis of depth of experience in the three areas of new product development, marketing, and management.

In the unlikely situation in which several candidates show up with equally high rankings, one can consider salary advantages that accrue from selecting the lowest priced candidate, length of service that may accrue from selecting the youngest candidate, and the pertinence of the formal training of the candidates.

"Value added" should be the controlling criterion in thinking about the services to be bought by the buyer. One's expectations of specific characteristics that add up to top performance in a manager's purview should be the characteristics one wants to buy. Nothing else is more important. If these are delivered by the chosen one, what else could the buyer want?

Thinking should be directed at what one does want not at what one does not want. The general applicable rule is: Don't select by eliminating negatives; add up the positives. To this rule there is no waiver. Accentuate the positive not the negative. Select by summing up the positives not by eliminating the negatives.

FINALIZING WHILE IN DOUBT

Doubts about the man picked for the job are symptomatic of unfinished business. The prognosis is trouble ahead. The diagnosis points to one or more of three functional failures: failure to develop a comprehensive and specific statement of the immediate and longer range nature of the job to be done, failure to adequately assess skills a man commands, failure to be effective in prospecting for prospects. In short doubts reflect failures in the process of picking the man for the job.

In filling a spot in his organization one executive commented to an associate, "I've finally, but reluctantly, filled that job I've been trying to fill for the past few months. I just couldn't spend any more time looking for a man. I'm sure not happy with my choice. He may make out but I've got deep doubts, and they are getting deeper the longer I think about it. I'll give him just six months to prove himself or out he goes."

This executive is headed directly into trouble. There isn't any valid reason why positions can't be filled with the right man for the job, the right man in every respect. To do this, however, means that the process of picking the man for the job must be executed with competence and thoroughness.

The process commences with the development of a position profile. There is something fundamentally wrong with a position profile that demands a combination of capabilities that are so esoteric that candidates can't be located. Doubts about the man may be traceable to a demand for a combination of capabilities that are rarely encountered. Such rare birds call for costly searches, and these rare birds, once found, command salaries out of reach. Yet, any candidate having capabilities that fall short of the rare bird required causes doubts to arise about his ability to do the job. When doubts arise, don't hire. Take another look at the position profile. Doubts traceable to esoteric position profiles can be remedied by restructuring the profile.

For example, Einsteins, Edisons, and Eastmans may be the men you want for the research job, but the more realistic approach is to combine talents through a research team approach. This is the alternative to a search for genius. You may want a manufacturing manager who can also design and sell, but are you willing to pay the cost of the search and salary of this talented individual? The better course of action is to restructure the function and position profile.

Once you have assured yourself that you are working with a realistic position profile, doubts due to this source can be eliminated. Next the focus shifts to the capabilities the man commands. If the position profile provides a comprehensive and specific statement of the immediate and longer range nature of the job to be done, working specifications are established. A review of prospects' past performance should separate the men with proved ability to do the job from those without proved ability to do the job.

Doubt in the mind of a manager may arise from reluctance to surrender responsibility. These managers know they can do the job better than anyone else. And they will not admit that any man can measure up to them in performance on the job. No candidate's credentials will surmount this hurdle when it exists. Doubts less egocentrically based suggest that the candidate's track record for performance hasn't been adequately assessed.

Did he or did he not perform in the past? Did he or did he not perform in a working environment comparable to the one in which he will be expected to perform? These and other questions should be asked in reviewing the record to remove doubts.

When it appears that his performance was not up to the level of the position to be filled, the prospect is not a candidate for the position. At this point doubts with respect to this prospect are removed. On the other hand his performance in the past may match the requirements of the position to be filled, thus placing him in the candidate category. However, doubts may arise as to whether or not other prospects might have done an even better job in the past and will do a better job in the future.

In other words, you wonder whether or not you have located the best of all men who could do the job. At this point a manager must face up to the fact that he will never know the answer to this question. When doubts remain at this point, the only thing to do is to continue the search and screening of candidates. As this goes on a manager will gain confidence in the rightness of his selection. Doubts as to his selection should diminish, but he will never know whether the man is really the best man he could have found had he searched for a longer time.

Hazards lurk here, too. The longer he searches the greater the cost in time, effort, and money both in the search and in lost performance in the unfilled position. Another hazard results from the risk inherent in overstaffing the assignment with a man who can do more than the job demands. Top performers won't waste their time on trivial assignments. In continuing to search for the best man, because of lingering doubts, managers run the risk of overselling the assignment. Candidates lured into this trap soon move to other organizations and assignments where their talents find a ready market.

Doubts remaining after reassessing the position profile and the prospect's performance record can be resolved by reassessing the competence and thoroughness of the search for candidates. When position profiles are realistic and prospects fail to measure up to performance specifications, don't give

up but don't hire; it is time to take a look at the search pro-
cedure itself.

As stated earlier, there isn't any valid reason why positions
can't be filled with the right man for the job, but he must be
located. Then he must be sold the assignment. He will only
accept a new assignment which provides him plus factors
going beyond his present assignment. These must be developed, established, and negotiated. Finally, he must be
sold to the new group with whom he will work. All of this is
part of the process of picking the man for the job. Done competently, doubts disappear. When doubts remain after looking at position profiles and prospects, don't hire but don't just
resume the search doing more of the same. Reassess the competence and thoroughness of the search itself.

The general applicable rule is: Don't employ when in
doubt; act on conviction not in desperation. To this there is
one waiver. When the situation demands action, compromises may be necessary. When this is the case, one should be
convinced that the urgency of the need to fill positions with
men who don't command the capabilities jobs demand more
than offsets resulting low levels of performance effectiveness.

The best course of action to take, when the urgency of the
situation demands that a position be filled with a candidate
whose capabilities fall short of those the job demands, is to
tailor the assignment to fit the man's capabilities. Why give
men things to do you don't think they can do? You'll waste
time looking over their shoulder anyway. Rebuild the job
around functions you are confident the candidate can cope
with competently.

Use the time you would otherwise waste double-checking
his work to assume part of the work left over as result of the
restructured assignment. Some functions can be shifted to
others. Now, one can go to work with confidence that tasks as
deployed will be executed competently. This approach re-

flects a compromise with the fundamentals of functional organization but, remember, staffing involved a compromise, too. Urgency dictated action.

There is another reason why men should not be given things to do a manager doesn't think they are capable of performing. Confidence is contagious. Lack of confidence is equally contagious. When W. J. told his personnel manager, "I've decided to give Bill a chance at the job as salesman in the Southwest territory even though I have a lot of doubts about his ability to make the grade," W. J. was starting to undermine Bill's performance before he had an opportunity to perform.

When a manager doesn't show confidence in a man, word gets around fast. No man can even begin to perform effectively when his every act is suspect from the start. Secretaries, associates, and others sense that he may not be around long. Telephone calls to the boss are given low priority and blocked by the boss's secretary. His reports are placed at the bottom of the pile. His every act is suspect. Requests for staff support are neglected. A man can't act effectively in such a situation.

In contrast, consider a second situation. Here in placing a man on an assignment, a manager doesn't say, "I doubt Bill can do the job. I'll give him six months to prove himself or out he goes." Rather, he says, "Bill is going to take over the Southwest territory, one of our most important territories. Bill's appointment brings new talent onto the job, talent I expect will rapidly carry Bill to much more important assignments in the near future."

Now, Bill will be given extra attention by everyone. His requests for support will be given immediate attention. His calls will go through promptly, and his reports will be placed on the top of the pile.

The fair-haired boy may even get too much support, to the extent that in some situation his mistakes are corrected or buried by others. As a result of always "smelling like a rose," the fair-haired boy is pushed upward beyond his capabilities, while other highly competent performers are held down.

Starting under a cloud of doubts, some good performers have erased initial doubts in the minds of managers who put them on trial but word of this vote of confidence by the boss has not always been communicated to others. As a consequence, these men continue to be regarded as men who aren't in favor with the boss and must continue to surmount invisible hurdles.

Little things can undermine overall organizational effectiveness. Don't add to them by hiring when in doubt. Unless the candidate can be given a clean bill of health, a vote of confidence, and enthusiastic support, find the man who qualifies for an introduction with kudos that will carry him forward with the full support of those with whom he must work.

PROBLEMS OR PERFORMANCE

Why do managers make these mistakes in picking the man for the job? To find an answer to this question, review the common mistakes managers make. The seven are these:

1. Attempting to fit the misfit.
2. Mistaking efficiency for effectiveness.
3. Expecting weaknesses to disappear.
4. Anticipating turnabouts.
5. Searching for Number Two.
6. Selecting by eliminating negatives.
7. Finalizing while in doubt.

Managers are made or broken by men who report to them. Yet, many managers assign a low priority to the function of searching, screening, and selecting the men through whom they must work to achieve their goals. As a consequence, these managers pay a high price. When men do not command capabilities jobs demand, problems multiply.

The experienced and effective manager knows that there is nothing more important than putting the right man on the right job at the right time. He knows that this is the most important thing he does. He knows that performance starts with sound staffing, and he knows that problems start with careless or hasty staffing. He assigns top priority to the staffing function.

Part III
Selecting

6

PICKING PRIME MOVERS

WITHIN 25 years after college, Norm had been a corporation president and a board member of several corporations. Now he is heading up a consulting group he organized. Steve had followed a different course of action. He has been a partner in a brokerage firm on Wall Street and a member of the New York Stock Exchange. A third man, George, headed up quality control at an outlying subsidiary of a multidivisional manufacturing organization.

Norm, Steve, and George all graduated from business school together. All three were in the top tenth of their class, and all three spent their first five years after graduation in the financial section of a major corporation where George is still working while Norm and Steve went on to better things.

Why? What distinguished Norm and Steve from George? How do you sort the men who can make things happen, who are able to adapt to change and to grow with the times, from those who don't make things happen? How do you identify the prime movers at an early date?

Managers are asking these questions. They know that their own success depends on their ability to spot men on the move, the men who are sensitive to situations and can capitalize on opportunities.

In an interview men will almost always present themselves as personally responsible for the things that are done. The problem is, "How can managers probe beneath the to-be-expected veneer of a candidate's self-embellishment to determine whether or not a man is the driver of the team or is going along for the ride?" For those willing to work at making interviews meaningful, where there is a will, there is a way to identify the prime movers.

No secrets underlie the approach successful managers use. Rather, success is based on the stark simplicity of the fact that the prime mover is always the man with a plan. He has fitted the pieces of the action together to take him where he wants to go. The problem is to identify the man with a plan.

To identify these men probing questions, put in proper order, have proved useful time and time again in revealing the men who are sensitive to the situation in which they find themselves and who know how to capitalize on opportunities. Answers to these questions identify the prime mover, the man who is going to grow, the man with a plan.

The first question to ask a candidate is, "What have you done recently to become more effective in your present position?" Too often, in interviewing a candidate a manager will make the mistake of saying to a man, "Tell me about yourself." The trouble with this approach is that it is one of the world's best ways to waste everyone's time. The interviewer should already know the things a candidate's going to tell him.

Highly qualified candidates learn more about those who are interviewing them than the interviewers learn about the candidates on many occasions. Meaningless and senseless time-consuming questions tell candidates that a manager doesn't know how to pick top performers. This scares good men away. They don't want to team up with managers who don't know how to pick men. The "Tell me about yourself," approach is one of the clues that alert candidates to the possibility that they had better avoid involvement with an organization.

The better question is, "What have you done recently to become more effective in your present position?" Time is being taken to interview the candidate, because it has already been established from a review of his past performance record that he has done things of interest. The purpose now is to determine whether or not he is a prime mover in the things that were done. The prime mover can talk about what he has done recently to become more effective in his present position, because he is the man who has initiated the action.

What distinguishes the prime mover on the job from his associates? To start with, the prime mover knows that no job is performed in a static setting. He knows that all functions are part of a changing and rapidly expanding economy. He intends to play a prominent part in this changing picture.

Others, the nonprime movers, make the mistake of seeing their jobs in a static setting. Left alone, these men never make changes in the things they are doing. They are sincere in their belief that they should do things the way that they have always been done. Policies, rules, and procedures dictate the way things should be done, and to question these dictates, let alone to suggest changes, deviates from these dictates and constitutes a breech of etiquette.

These are the men who always fall back on the rules to justify their action when things they have done have created brush fires for managers to extinguish. There will be a never-ending succession of brush fires for managers to put out as long as managers have men around who attempt to maintain a static setting in a dynamic environment.

The prime mover, on the other hand, recognizes that

policies, rules, and procedures were tailored to yesterday's activities. In everything he does, he is sensitive to the changing situation, and he capitalizes on opportunities. Change shows up in different ways. Ups and downs occur in the economy. A swing either way creates opportunities for those who are sensitive to the situation. New technologies, legislative enactments, market shifts, and so on, all create, reflect, or respond in themselves to change and new opportunities arise.

Wherever he is and whatever he is doing, the prime mover is sensitive to changes that have an impact on his activities. The action he takes is suited to the situation in which he finds himself. Under one set of circumstances, he may suggest a change in the course of action to the manager to whom he reports. In another situation, he may initiate a change in the action himself.

His proposals won't always be accepted, and he must learn to accept criticism because he has done things in new and different ways. He even runs the risk of being fired. The prime mover accepts these facts of life. He would rather be fired for doing things to become more effective on the job than to run the risk of being part of a static setting.

Every day, organizations are closing their doors because managers failed to respond to change. These are the managers who fired the prime movers. Each time these organizations close their doors, they put on the street loyal and faithful servants who have impressive service records and titles. These men weren't fired for doing new and different things. They did things as they had always been done. That is why they and their associates are looking for work.

When the interviewer encourages a man to talk about the things he has done to become more effective in his present position, he can find out whether the man is sensitive to change and knows how to plan to capitalize on opportunities created by change. When a man can't talk about the changes he has made in his job to become more effective on the job, it is a clear indicator that he isn't driving the team but, rather, is going along for the ride. This response tells the manager that this man will not assume any responsibility himself. The manager will not be able to multiply his effectiveness through the eyes and ears of this man.

Few managers can afford to limit their effectiveness by selecting men who aren't sensitive to the situation and who can't capitalize on opportunities. Times are changing too rapidly today for one man to assume responsibility in any group.

A word of warning: Ask a man to talk about the things he has done to become more effective on the job as part of the interview. Don't make this question part of a background information form. The man who has done significant things can talk about them without hesitation. The man who hasn't made contributions to his assignment will find himself at a disadvantage. He is prepared to talk about things he does but not about changes he has made in his job. He won't have time to fabricate changes. When the question appears on a written form it alerts a man and gives him an opportunity to fabricate answers to an obviously significant question.

Past performance records should reveal prime movers, but to sharpen the focus questions asked during discussions with candidates should be of an offbeat nature, questions forcing candidates to be candid in their remarks to the degree that questions are unanticipated.

The second question to ask is, "How much of your own money have you invested in your personal development in the past twelve months and for what specific purposes?" Again, ask the question during an interview. Don't make it part of a written background information form. There isn't any one right answer to this question but there is an underlying concept that is revealing.

To illustrate this second question, one man, Ed, replied,

"Not a dollar. Didn't have to. My company has an educational fund. It's available to anyone. All that we need to do is to submit a request for funding for a course of study reasonably related to a proposed personal development plan that appears feasible within the company or one related to a need to prepare for changing requirements in our present assignment. Once approved, half of the money is advanced without any strings attached. We get the rest when, and if, we complete parts of the program with passing grades. During the past year, I have been taking a tax course and one in international law since we are expanding our overseas operations."

Ed was fortunate. There was no need for him to invest his own money in his personal development, but he recognized the need for a personal development program to prepare himself for things that lay ahead. Some men never seem to recognize that there is an expiration date on every diploma.

Most men must spend some of their own money if they want to renew the date on their diploma. This does not appear to be an unreasonable requirement. A conservative estimate of the cost of a college education, taking into consideration out of pocket costs and lost earnings for four years, is $30,000. This asset is subject to a rapid rate of depreciation for a number of reasons.

No job a graduate accepts will make use of all of the knowledge and skills he has at his command at graduation. Some knowledge and skills will be used more than others; some won't be needed immediately, but will be needed later. Through lack of use, knowledge and skills are lost unless a man plans a personal development program that will help him maintain capabilities he will need at a future time to present a competitive posture among his peers. This is just one aspect of the impact of depreciation on an individual's investment in an education.

A second aspect arises as a result of advancing technology in every area of man's activities. Yesterday's best way of doing things gives way to new and better ways, as new approaches, systems, and technologies are developed. Just because a man is applying his knowledge and skills on his assignment is no assurance that he is making use of the newest and best approaches. The only way he can be sure is to set aside time for study of new developments in areas of activity of importance to him.

Some men seem to wear blinders. They can see only what they are doing. They concentrate only on doing more of the same. Their efficiency may be on the increase while their effectiveness is decreasing, because new technologies replace their way of working. For example, computers have replaced bookkeepers, but alert men, those sensitive to the situation, have developed new skills and multiplied their effectiveness. These men weren't replaced by computers; the computers report to them. However, men only maintain a competitive posture when they plan personal development programs permitting them to maintain such a posture among their peers.

A third aspect of the depreciation of a man's knowledge and skills men must face up to is the fact that from time to time they must write off knowledge and skills they no longer need. As men move ahead and accept more senior assignments, they must leave earlier assignments to others. Acceptance of this fact should be reflected in a man's personal development program.

Some men never want to let go of their last job when an opportunity to move ahead arises. They want to remain on top of everything. They are reluctant to let men who report to them become the experts on their former assignments. Fearful lest they will lose the respect of these men, they try to run two jobs. Yet, these same men are resentful when the man to whom they report thinks the same way and holds them back by refusing to surrender the expertise while running their jobs.

These men pursue a personal development program with a vengeance, trying to update themselves in technologies which should be surrendered to juniors. It is just as important to spot the man whose personal development program is cluttered with things he shouldn't be doing as it is to identify the men who have a well-planned personal development program. Continuing education isn't what one is looking for in identifying the prime movers. One is looking for the men who have planned, selectively, to develop in directions in which they should be developing to capitalize on opportunities.

A man's development program should reflect sensitivity and selectivity. It should reflect sensitivity to maintain and develop knowledge and skills that will be needed at some future time in his career. It should also reflect sensitivity to a need to develop a familiarity with changing technologies related to his present assignment and his willingness to let some skills become obsolete on a selective basis.

Depending on his assignment, the drop-off in the range of a man's knowledge and skills is somewhere between 10 and 20 percent a year unless he plans a program to refurbish and develop his capabilities. To maintain the level, range, and up-to-date nature of the knowledge and skills he had at graduation, a man would have to spend more time on a personal development program than any job would ever permit.

The answer to this seeming dilemma lies in the fact that it wouldn't be worth the effort. At the time of graduation a man has completed a training program purposely designed to be broad in scope because he has not chosen a career path. As his interests develop with the passing of time and as opportunities become clearer, his development program should reflect sensitivity to the needs of an elected career. The value of knowledge and skills is measured by utility not quantity.

The prime movers aren't the men who know more than other men. They know less. It isn't really necessary to know much. The man who knows the most is suspect of not knowing his needs. He must know what knowledge he needs and where to get it.

Men tend to fall short in learning how to learn and what to learn. The emphasis isn't on continuing education; it is on being able to select appropriate education and learning how to learn. Prime movers are aware of this. Their personal development programs reflect it. Development programs built around these three attributes prepare men to adapt to change and to grow by maintaining a sensitivity to the situation and by capitalizing on opportunity.

A man's lifetime earnings range from less than half a million dollars to a million dollars or more. Regardless of the amount, a portion of this money should be invested to offset the continuing depreciation of his knowledge and skills asset. A man should be able to make a good accounting of his personal development plans. The prime mover is identified by the fact that he is a man with a plan.

The third question to ask is, "How do you evaluate your effectiveness?" What men say in response to this question tells managers whether men can distinguish the difference between efficiency and effectiveness.

When asked this question, Bob replied, "I measure my effectiveness on the basis of how hard and long I work. I keep more than busy all of the time. I can always find things to do. Not only that, I work overtime and frequently on Saturdays. I am not afraid of work. When others are overloaded, I'm the man they come to for help."

Bob's belief that hard work and long hours reflect a measure of a man's effectiveness is a belief shared by many men. Men who think this way work this way—long and hard. Some men work two shifts, but this doesn't reflect either efficiency or effectiveness.

There is nothing wrong with putting in a long day and applying oneself to the job. This is to be commended provided one is doing worthwhile things. However, little is to be gained in a long day of hard work when what one is doing isn't worthwhile.

Men make a common mistake of getting so involved in what they are doing and the way they are doing it that they fail to check to be certain that they are doing the most worthwhile thing they could be doing with their time, energy, and other resources. These men's desks are piled high with papers. It is difficult to get to see them. Their appointment list is long. Their brief cases bulge with papers when they leave in the evening, but all of this tells nothing about their effectiveness for one simple reason. Doing more and better what one is doing isn't worthwhile when what one is doing isn't worthwhile.

In asking a man how he evaluates his effectiveness, one should listen for replies that focus on the worthwhileness of the end results of the man's activity.

When Dave was asked the same question, he replied, "I measure my effectiveness three ways. First, the things I am doing should be accelerating my organization's movement towards its goals. Second, the things I am doing should be moving me towards my own goals as rapidly as possible. Third, the things I am doing should be done in new and better ways geared to changes taking place all the time and to the opportunities associated with these changes."

Dave knows the difference between effectiveness and efficiency. Dave is end-results oriented. He knows that it isn't the means but the ends that count. His thinking is oriented toward opportunity and results.

Every so often one wonders why one man seems to be so successful while working so little while another man grinds away and gets nowhere. The reason is quite simple. One man does things that are worthwhile; the other does things to which little or no value is attached.

Everyone recognizes that digging ditches will never be as rewarding as piloting a commercial airplane, but men overlook subtle differences in their activities that spell the difference between what is worthwhile and what isn't worthwhile.

In answering the question, "How do you evaluate your effectiveness?" the prime mover will make it clearly apparent that he measures effectiveness in terms of the worthwhileness of the end results of his activities. He doesn't confuse the means to the end with the end itself. He never talks about hard work and long hours. The prime mover doesn't work hard or work long hours. It isn't necessary. Men who do worthwhile things in worthwhile ways don't have to work hard or work long hours.

A *fourth question* to ask is, "Where do you want to be positioned in the future in terms of responsibilities and rewards?" What one replies reveals a number of significant things.

First, these replies reveal whether or not those questioned have thought about their future. Most men don't give any serious constructive thought to their future. The man who says something such as, "Well I expect to move up in position and salary," hasn't given any thought to his future. His is just voicing his hopes.

Promotions and salary increases will be reflections of a man's increased capabilities to the organization. These increased capabilities, in turn, will reflect constructive thought about the future.

The man who has thought about the future will talk in terms of the moves he is planning to make from where he is to where he wants to go to do the things he wants to do in the future.

When Ned was asked where he wanted to be positioned in the future, he replied, "I usually shake up my associates when I talk about my future in the company."

"Why so?" asked Ray, the manager interviewing Ned.

"Primarily because by the time I move along and up I expect to see us in a very different kind of business. We aren't going to be doing the things that are important to us today. As a result, I believe that we will have a different organizational structure. For example, I think we are going to centralize many of the administrative and sales operations that now report to our product divisions. This is going to create a top policy level position as vice president and director of information resource systems, and I'm setting my sights on that position. I want to be responsible for developing information systems that will free managers from the responsibility for routine decision making by having decisions made before the fact rather than after the fact."

"I'll have to admit that for the moment I feel a bit shaken up, too, Ned. I expected that you would see only yourself moving ahead, not the whole organization. But you are right; nothing stands still. Things move ahead or fall behind," replied Ray.

This discussion between Ned and Ray highlights the second significant aspect of men's replies when asked where they want to be positioned in the future. Not only does one want to know whether or not a man has thought about the future but one wants to know how he visualizes the future itself. Does he see the future as merely a projection of the past?

Men make a common mistake of visualizing the future as if they were peering through a large magnifying glass at the present. Things are all in the same relative relationship; it is just that everything is bigger. As a consequence, any plans these men make will not enable them to attain viable goals. Even the best thought-out plans by men who do view a changed future run the risk of taking men down the wrong road.

This risk highlights a third significant aspect of the replies of those questioned. Their thoughts about the future should incorporate flexibility. Plans shouldn't be too rigid. They should allow for course changes as the future unfolds. Men who overplan run the risk that their plans will take them where they won't want to be when they get there because personal interests or opportunities have changed.

Plans cannot be too tightly formulated. Such planning isn't easily shifted into new patterns when interests and opportunities change. Prime movers, on the contrary, have plans for the future. While they do visualize a future in which things look different from the way they look today, prime movers are ready to change their plans. They want to capitalize on new and better opportunities as they become apparent with the passing of time.

A *fifth question* to ask candidates is, "Do you get good support for the things you want to do?" When asked this question, Mike replied, "No, it's an uphill fight all the way."

"Why?" asked Neil who was interviewing Mike as a candidate for a new assignment.

"For one thing, no one understands the things I'm doing?"

"Don't you discuss your plans and get general approval before you get going in a particular direction?"

"How can I do that? I don't know myself from day to day. Things keep shifting. I just have to cope with things on a hand-to-mouth basis putting out brush fires."

"But don't you have any plans to eliminate these brush fires?"

"No. I'm too busy to do any planning."

"Doesn't this situation concern your superior?"

"I don't know. If it does he hasn't said so."

In responding to the question, "Do you get good support for the things you want to do?" and guided by Neil's skillful questioning, Mike has proved that he can't be classified among the prime movers.

First, Mike admits that he hasn't any immediate objectives. The words "too busy," "don't know myself from day to day," "hand-to-mouth," and "brush fires" identify him without even short-range goals. The men who don't know what they are going to try to accomplish on a day-to-day basis aren't going to accomplish much compared with men who have established immediate goals. Face it, the man who isn't trying to do anything constructive isn't going to do anything constructive.

Second, Mike's comment "No one understands the things I'm doing" says volumes about his candidacy. How can anyone understand what Mike is doing when Mike admits "I don't know myself. Things keep shifting."

A second candidate, Burt, gave a different reply to Neil's question, "Do you get good support for the things you want to do?"

When asked this question, Burt smiled and replied, "Not as good as I'd like, but then everyone wants his needs satisfied, and there isn't enough money to go around. However, I do get good moral support."

"To what do you attribute your success?"

"Sound strategy," replied Burt. "I try to think along with the boss. After all, he has a pipeline to the top. I know I'm going to get whatever support I do get when I do things top management wants done. Of course, I try to mold their thinking by injecting ideas of my own. I play a little game with management. I call it "Trade-off." I let them win most of the time and, in turn, they let me win once in a while."

Burt gets good support for the things he wants to do for four apparent reasons. He takes time to establish good rapport with the man to whom he reports. He keeps posted on management's primary interests. He sells his ideas to management. He makes his plans coincide with management thinking. Burt is a prime mover.

Men are in trouble when others don't have a clear understanding of what they are trying to do. Their troubles are compounded when they themselves don't know what they are trying to do. That is, they don't have any day-to-day plans of their own. The man who is too busy putting out brush fires to take time to plan his day will always be confronted with more brush fires than he can ever handle. Men like this never become prime movers.

The sixth question to ask is, "What use are you making of your knowledge of yourself?" This question has a host of familiar questions rolled up into one. Because of this it reveals a man's thinking about himself better than individual questions that are often asked to arrive at the answer to this basic question.

The man who responds by asking, "What do you mean?" is telling an interviewer that he isn't making any use of his knowledge of himself because he hasn't tried to know himself. The man who tries to know himself has done so to capitalize and improve on his competitive posture.

Prime movers don't ask "What do you mean?" They know what you mean. They have already asked questions of themselves to identify their strengths, weaknesses, interests, and resources. Beyond asking questions, they have taken steps to improve their competitive posture.

Prime movers are opportunists. They capitalize on their strengths and avoid things that highlight their weaknesses. One man commented, "I know that I'm not good at figures. I never was good at figures, but I figured out one thing. I can sell ideas to others. Rather than wasting my time strengthening my weaknesses with figures, I have spent my time doing things where I can work with people, because I can get people to do things for me."

One of the reasons why so many people seek private counseling services today is because they are overly concerned about their weaknesses. The prime mover thinks positively. He thinks about his strengths and how he can develop his strengths and put them to work for him in ways in which his weaknesses will not enter the picture. No one is without weaknesses, but when men avoid doing things that call attention to weaknesses, weaknesses cease to be problems.

The important thing is to identify strengths and work on

the development of strengths. Anyway you look at it, a 10 percent improvement in an area of strength is a greater aggregate performance improvement than a 10 percent improvement in an area of weakness. The only time attention should be given to a weakness is when this weakness blocks the exercise of strength. Otherwise, forget the weakness.

Many men neglect an important aspect of knowing themselves. They overlook and even fail to recognize their resources. Every man has resources at his disposal. For some, it is money, an extremely valuable resource. For others, it is a commanding appearance. Some are talented. Knowing the right people, a winning personality, and family connections are all resources.

You must know your resources. Then, you must know when to capitalize on your resources and when it is not to your advantage to capitalize on a particular resource. Finally, you must act at the right time and follow through in capitalizing on a resource.

Ask the prime mover, "What use are you making of your knowledge of yourself?" and he won't reply, "What do you mean?" He will have something to say. He will tell you about his strengths and what he is doing to develop them, and about his resources and how he is using them. You won't hear much about his weaknesses. While he avoids them, he recognizes them and will talk about them, too, if pressed to do so.

Finally, there is a fourth facet of his knowledge of himself he can talk about. He knows his interests. He knows what he likes and what he doesn't like. He makes good use of this knowledge of his interests in capitalizing on his strengths and resources and in side-stepping his weaknesses. He knows men do their best when they are doing things they like to do. In every respect the prime mover is making good use of his knowledge of himself.

A *seventh question* to ask a man is, "What is your attitude towards responsibilities, risk, and rewards?" Listen to some answers to this question.

BOYD: I'm no gambler. You can depend on me to follow the rules. No one can complain that I didn't do what I was told to do. If there is any question about what should be done I kick the question upstairs. It's my boss's responsibility to make the decision.

SAM: To be frank, I take a lot of chances. I know the policy manual says this and that, but that's a book for the fellows who don't have any get up and go. If we are going to move ahead in my division we have got to compete with the brass knuckles on. My salary is tied to our profit picture. If I improve profits, nobody is going to object to the methods I used.

Look at it this way. It is clearly my responsibility to improve profits. Rewards are based on performance. I'll never make a showing if I don't take some risks. That sums up my philosophy with respect to responsibilities, risk, and rewards.

WALTER: I faced the problem of how to relate responsibilities, risk, and rewards when I took over my present job. Up until that time, I didn't really have an opportunity to run risks, because I was just a straw boss. In my new job it was different; I can take some chances. I sat down with my boss at the start and asked him just how close he wanted me to stick to the letter of the law, where he wanted me to stretch the rules, and what things he wanted to handle himself.

He said the responsibility for doing my job was mine but that he would discuss any matter I wanted to talk over with him at any time. Further, he pointed out that our operating procedures reflect experience of the past in dealing with our affairs on a best-way basis. This did not mean that these procedures would apply on a best-way basis as conditions changed. He pointed out that as situations changed it could be a serious mistake to cling to old ways. At the same time one would be sticking one's neck out in departing from established policies and that one's neck could be chopped off.

Based on this, I feel that it is my responsibility to exercise judgment in coping with changed conditions. To do this I must accept risk.

ROY: It seems to me that the whole relationship between responsibilities, risk, and rewards can be summed up simply. No one can ever wait until he has all the facts needed to act without running risks. If a man didn't run risks he'd be stopped dead in his tracks unless he had some menial job. Since a man won't get paid unless he does something, he's got to take risks; it is that simple.

JIM: I try to relate risk to my degree of responsibility to others and the nature of my responsibility to others. For example, in the handling of the company's property, it is my responsibility to act in a fiduciary relationship. I am a trustee. I should protect that property and reduce risk of loss to the lowest level possible.

On the other hand, in sales negotiations, I am dealing with uncertainties. When I promise early delivery of merchandise, we get orders we would lose to others if I didn't gamble on our ability to make delivery and escape the penalty charges for late delivery. Here it is my responsibility to run risk.

To turn the situation around, I could cut our property insurance and save money, but I'd run the risk of losses. In sales, I could refuse to accept delivery risks and accept only the orders we could be sure of delivering on time.

Acceptance of risk involves judgment between fiduciary and profit-building responsibilities.

Now, who is right and who is wrong? Four of these men, Sam, Walter, Roy, and Jim are counted among the prime movers. Boyd is the dropout. Someone has said, "Rules are made for fools to follow." While it is an overstatement of fact, rules are made to be broken when conditions surrounding rules change. Prime movers weigh their responsibilities, analyze the risks, assess the rewards, and act accordingly. Those who feel that this leaves much to be desired as a guideline are correct; it does. Those who expect more specific guidelines as a basis for their actions shouldn't be asking these seven questions.

These seven questions tell the skilled observer things he needs to know to separate the men who make things happen from the men who are victims of happenings. These are probing questions without being leading questions. They ask a man questions without suggesting that there are right answers.

There aren't any right answers. The skilled interviewer must assess the significance of a man's experience and job knowledge, his ability to conceptualize, and his ability to handle himself in the environment in which the action is to be carried out. Answers to these questions reveal these characteristics, but beyond this they reveal the men who are sensitive to situations, who make things happen, adapt to change, capitalize on opportunities, and grow—in short, the prime movers.

7

IDENTIFYING GROWTH POTENTIAL

"Two prospects look outstanding, based on past performance, but how do you tell whether one of them has reached his peak and is beginning to level off?" asked a manager who had a key position to fill, one which demanded growth potential.

There are no answers to these questions that can be applied in all cases. Individuals are just that, individuals. But good guidelines can be given those managers who are willing to take the time to weigh and assess the pieces of the action.

In all the pieces of the action, there is one common denominator: achievement. *Actions speak louder than words, but achievements speak louder than actions.* In each of the action areas, achievement is the measure of the effectiveness of the action, and the "how" of the achievement reveals a man's potential as a future achiever.

Every man can point to some achievement, modest though his achievement may be. Digging a ditch is an achievement for one man. Another man can point to having dug a ditch and erected forms for concrete foundations. Still another is a teller in a bank. A fourth man is an accountant, and so it goes.

Each achievement is a measure of the effectiveness of the action. Achievements establish present proficiency levels but alert managers look ahead. They know times will change, and they want to surround themselves with men who can adapt to change and grow with the times. These managers are interested in a prospect's growth potential.

Figure 7–1
ACHIEVEMENT TREND LINES

Up to some point everyone "grows." That is, one's proficiency level rises as shown in Figure 7–1. But it is equally true that at some point one's proficiency buildup ceases. When this occurs, one's proficiency level falls. One ages rather than grows.

This, of course, begs the question, "Can't a man maintain a proficiency level without growing or aging?" It should be possible, but the experience of the past reveals that men either grow or age on the job. Men who can adjust to the changing demands of their assignments just don't stand still.

They grow. In picking the man for the job, you are looking for men who are going to grow rather than age.

"If achievement is the common denominator in the pieces of the action in a man's performance," managers ask, "what aspect of achievement reveals a man's growth potential? Or, what signals the commencement of aging?"

The experience of the past suggests that no one thing will alert a manager to growth potential or to the fact that aging has commenced. On the other hand a number of things taken together separate men with growth potential from those who are aging.

To start with, achievement results from the application of effort. A simple action analogue, shown in Figure 7–2, illus-

Figure 7–2
ACTION ANALOGUE

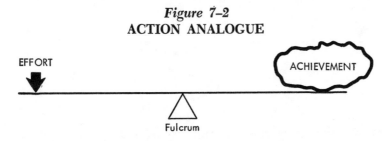

trates the relationships involved. Effort applied on one side of the fulcrum is reflected in a matching achievement on the other side of the fulcrum.

Hard workers won't dispute the logic of this simple action analogue. Nor do they dispute the fact that to increase the magnitude of the achievement one must exert a greater effort. You witness examples of this daily when you hear these men talk about how hard they work.

Hard workers work—and, more significantly, think—in a one-to-one frame of reference. This is what wears them out. These men think that to double their output they must double their effort. This kind of thinking separates these men from others with growth potential.

One can't argue that the 1:1 performers don't increase the magnitude of their achievement through the application of greater effort, but hard work is the slow way to raise achievement levels.

Be on the lookout for the man who goes to work earlier and earlier and comes home later and later. Be on the lookout for the man whose home becomes a second office on nights and weekends. Be on the lookout for the man who is too busy to take vacations. Be on the lookout for the man who

Figure 7–3
ACTION ADVANTAGE

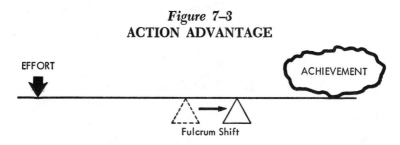

is taking efficiency courses such as speed reading. And be on the lookout for the man who is "tired" at the end of the day.

In short, be on the lookout for the 1:1 performers, the men who are following the more-of-the-same route to greater achievement. These men are hard workers.

Longer hours and increased efficiency spell hard work. Hard work will lead to greater achievement. Unfortunately for the men who are following the hard work route to greater achievement, they must operate in a competitive environment. The 1:1 effort-to-achievement ratio isn't good enough. When others do more, the 1:1 performers appear to be standing still or losing ground. This is just one of the facts of life that must be accepted by all men who work in a competitive environment.

Men who demonstrate real growth potential don't think in a 1:1 frame of reference. For these men it is more of a 1:10 or 1:100 frame of reference. To increase their achievements, these men don't work harder, they work more intelligently. What is their secret? They have discovered leverage.

These men shift the fulcrum toward the achievement end of the action analogue as shown in Figure 7–3. They capitalize on added action advantage gained through leverage. They reduce their effort to a minimum in whatever they do. Then, they do more with less effort, because they multiply their effectiveness.

How do they do it? These fulcrum shifters work in many ways, ways which are revealed by the pieces of the action. The ways of working of these fulcrum shifters gives managers good guidelines to use in weighing and assessing the pieces of the action to detect men with growth potential.

First, the pieces of the action of the fulcrum shifters reveal that these men have learned to learn. The statement, often heard, "He'll never learn," aptly describes the man who hasn't learned to learn.

When the pieces of the action don't reveal that a man is learning new things, growth can't continue. Change is continually taking place. Those who aren't learning new things can't participate in change. When men can't be part of change, growth stops.

Of course, at some time in his career, every individual has learned things, some more than others. The significant aspect of learning, however, is not how much a man has learned but how rapidly a man can learn.

For example, if A learns twice as rapidly as B, A can always know twice as much as B. A can always be ahead in any undertaking because A can learn things twice as rapidly as B.

Men with growth potential learn faster than others, because they don't waste time learning things they don't need to know. They identify things they need to know. Those who don't know what they need to know waste too much time learning things they don't need to know.

Most men know too much and not enough, at the same time. The aspect of learning that distinguishes the man who is growing from the man who is aging is the fact that the man who is growing has learned to learn the things he needs to know.

The man who is aging knows too much he doesn't need to know and not enough of what he needs to know. The man who is growing knows what he needs to know. He isn't weighted down and slowly sinking in a sea of knowledge much of which is useless to him today and all of which will be useless in the tomorrows.

The argument that grades tell nothing about a man is fallacious. Grades tell much about a man. Grades reveal a man's ability to acquire new know-how. Grades also reveal a man's ability to identify the things he needs to know to get good grades.

These two, the ability to learn new things and the ability to identify the things one needs to know, taken together, make up the significant measure of a man's ability to learn.

The pieces of the action reveal more than an ability to learn facts; the pieces of the action reveal a man's ability to learn new fundamentals, skills, techniques, concepts, viewpoints, and theories. All must be current, comprehensive, competent, and the best available anywhere if a prospect is to present himself in the best possible posture to a manager as a man possessing growth potential.

The men who have learned to learn exercise leverage. They can shift the fulcrum toward the achievement end of the action analogue and capitalize on action advantage to be gained through leverage. They reduce their effort to a minimum in whatever they do. Then, they do more, because they multiply their effectiveness. When the pieces of the action reveal that men have learned to learn, they reveal men with growth potential.

Second, the pieces of the action of the fulcrum shifters reveal that these men have done worthwhile things themselves. Men with growth potential have been aware that there is only one good reason for learning new things and that reason is to put this learning to good use. The pieces of the action reveal this. It's one of the ways these men shift the fulcrum, gain action advantage, and do more with less effort.

Most men don't put the things they know to work to good advantage. Because of this they can't grow. Men who grow know how to put to use the things they know. It is because of this that these men grow.

In picking men with growth potential, the pieces of the action should be examined to identify worthwhile contributions a man has made to activities to which he has been assigned. Many men do things but not worthwhile things. There is a difference between the two.

For example, in almost every organization there are men whose activities can't stand close scrutiny. These men talk a great deal about what is wrong with things and about how things should be done, but when you get right down to it they don't do things, and their activities consist largely of talk. Other men are busy, too; they spend much of their time writing papers, conducting meetings, attending conferences, and taking trips, but the net result of all of this adds up to motion, not things done.

In the pieces of the action of the men who have demonstrated growth in the past, there has been evidence of things done not just evidence of talk and motion. There have been tangible results of their efforts that one could point to, hold up, and examine. In the case of these men no one has ever asked, "What does he do all day?" The things they have done have been apparent to everyone.

Of course, even these doers have functioned in a competitive frame of reference. Things men do are relative; they are measured against the output of others. The fulcrum shifters check out with a high score. The quantitative as well as qualitative analysis of their achievements has been competitive with their contemporaries.

Just as the significant measure of learning has been the ability to learn new things and to identify the things one needs to know, the significant measure of the doing of worthwhile things is tangible evidence of relative productivity—evidence of competitiveness with contemporaries in terms of identifiable and measurable output.

Men who can't put know-how to work can't grow. Growth potential is reflected by the new and more worthwhile things men have done. Men who can't do worthwhile things don't grow. They don't have any launch pad for growth. Fulcrum shifters raise their levels of achievement by putting to use the things they know by doing worthwhile things.

Third, the pieces of the action of the fulcrum shifters reveal that these men have developed expertise. In what these men have done, they have excelled; they have soon established "best man" status. In examining the pieces of the action, it is evident that they were the leaders. Others have sought their advice and counsel and followed in their footsteps.

Someone once described a consultant as a man who steals your watch and tells you the time of day. Men with growth potential haven't been this kind of consultant. Men with growth potential have demonstrated real expertise by doing worthwhile things themselves and doing these things in better ways than others are doing them.

This expertise has enabled these men to shift the fulcrum further towards the achievement end of the action analogue to gain greater leverage.

Fourth, the pieces of the action of the fulcrum shifters re-

veal that these men have demonstrated management skills. The transition from "best man" posture to manager posture is a tough one for all men. Tougher than some can take but the evidence reveals that men with growth potential have made this transition with the characteristic ease with which they have done all things.

In fact, every man is a manager; he must manage himself. He can't sidestep this responsibility to himself. But beyond this point, many men run into a roadblock of their own making. As a result, they can't shift the fulcrum further and capitalize on the action advantage to be gained by working through others.

For the most part, fear itself is the roadblock. It is a twofold fear. Up to the time a man makes the transition from expert to manager, he lives in a right-wrong (R/W) environment. In this R/W environment there is a right way to do things and a wrong way to do things. As a learner, doer, or expert, men work in the R/W environment. The man who obeys the rules can do no wrong. This environment offers men security, but to become managers, they must surrender security.

The breakthrough one must make in becoming a manager involves a willingness to accept the risk of being wrong. There are no R/W rules for managers. In leaving the security of the R/W environment, managers enter a risk-reward (R/R) environment. In this R/R environment, the highest rewards are associated with the highest risks. Managers must make decisions based on probabilities. Men lacking the courage to back up their convictions don't survive as managers.

The second facet of the twofold fear that blocks a man from making the transition from expert to manager is the fear that he will no longer be looked up to as the expert; others will know more than he does. With respect to this, a manager need not fear it; he must accept it as a fact. He will no longer be an expert; he will, in fact and deed, from this point forward in his career, become a jack-of-all-trades, totally dependent on others for advice and counsel.

The men who have had growth potential have recognized that in making the breakthrough from expert to manager they gain more than they lose. This is a fundamental of growth, to gain more than is lost.

Managers gain the freedom and opportunity inherent in working in an R/R environment. In addition, no longer confined by the responsibility for maintaining an area of expertise, managers can draw on others for advice and counsel. In turn, managers put this knowledge to good use and provide support and growth opportunities for all involved.

In other words, growth-minded men have recognized that by becoming managers they have once more moved the fulcrum and increased the leverage. Nor have the growth-minded men stopped here.

Fifth, the pieces of the action of the fulcrum shifters reveal that these men have proved themselves as strategists. It is one more way growth-oriented men shift the fulcrum to multiply their effectiveness.

These men have recognized that to adapt to continuing changes taking place all of the time and to grow one must not only exercise control but have freedom to exercise control. As rapidly as was possible, growth-minded men have put themselves in a position where they have this freedom and control.

In a sense, strategists are managers' managers. The relationship is symbionic in nature and synergistic in effect. The strategist works through the manager, and the manager depends upon the strategist for direction; the output of the cooperative relationship is greater than would be possible without this working relationship.

Growth is based on capitalizing on opportunities created by change. Sensing change, spotting opportunities, defining goals, and formulating guidelines are four fundamental elements in the development of strategies. Once strategies have been developed, tacticians can go to work.

Men with growth potential have revealed their capabilities as strategists early in their careers. We are inclined to view the strategist as one sitting in a lofty post at the top of an organization where his pronouncements change the course of events for those below.

Some of us go further and regard those in high places as strategists. Not so. Too many of those in high places are neither strategists nor growth-minded men. There are ways in which men reach the top without qualifying as strategists. Family relationships and political "accidents," for example, are two of the most common ways in which men with pedestrian minds rise to rule at great cost to the organizations they rule.

Strategists are found at all levels in organizational hierarchies. The worker who senses an opportunity to act more effectively and plans a course of action to capitalize on this opportunity is a strategist just as much as those at higher levels. The impact of strategies developed at higher levels may be greater than the impact of those developed at lower levels, but strategists are nonetheless strategists wherever found.

As organizations grow in size, the volume of the work to be performed increases. Functional technicians and maintenance men must be moved along to process ongoing activities of the organization. Upward motion, however, should not be confused with growth potential. Many of these men are 1:1 thinkers, not men with growth potential. The 1:1 thinkers can cope with the increase in size and volume of things done today. They will do tomorrow what is being done today the way it is being done today, but someone else will have to show the way if new things are to be done to capitalize on change.

At all organizational levels, the growth-minded men have been called upon to show others the way to capitalize on opportunities. Examination of the pieces of the action reveals these men. They are the ones who have identified opportunities and initiated change. Depending upon their working level, they have done this in different ways.

Accountants may sense that management should have different data to be better informed of changes taking place. The strategists among them have planned programs to provide such data. Engineers who have been strategists have developed plans to eliminate tests made obsolete by the availability of better materials.

Regardless of the level at which men work, the pieces of the action reveal men's capability to identify opportunities and to initiate change, the ability to show others directions that will enable them to capitalize on change. Understandably, the pieces of the action that reveal men as strategists become more sophisticated as men move upward in the organization.

Regardless of the level at which men work, the pieces of the action reveal the men who can sense change, spot opportunities, and capitalize on change. Growth-oriented men have always done these things, because they recognize this to be one more way of shifting the fulcrum, of gaining action advantage and of multiplying the effectiveness of their efforts. They know it's the only way to grow.

Sixth, the pieces of the action of the fulcrum shifters reveal that these men have acted as innovators. Innovators exercise the greatest leverage of all. Strategists sense change. Innovators create change.

Innovators bridge the gap between ideas and reality. They create opportunities known only to them. By being first, they are in an enviable position to take advantage of opportunities they create. Men who do this multiply the effectiveness of their efforts many times.

Growth-oriented men have always been innovators. That is, they have done things that haven't been done before in the environment in which they work. Some of these men have done things that have never been done before. These men have been inventors. Other innovators, while not inventors, have pioneered the application of ideas of creators of new concepts.

All have initiated new and different concepts, turned ideas into reality, created change, created opportunities, and have capitalized on these opportunities. All, by exercising leverage, have multiplied their effectivness many times.

The Action Advantage

In every sense, achievement is a measure of the effectiveness of the action, but some men have greater growth potential than others. In tapping top talent, managers look for guidelines that will aid in identifying the men with the greatest growth potential.

The best clues are found in the pieces of the action that, put together, make up men's careers. In the past, and the past is prologue, the men who have adapted to change and have grown have been men who knew how to exercise leverage. These men have grown because by exercising leverage it was easier for them to do the things they did. Those who didn't know how to exercise leverage had to work harder.

Those who have aged early in their careers have had to work too hard to achieve the things they were able to achieve. They didn't know how to shift the fulcrum, multiply the effectiveness of their efforts, and work smarter not harder.

In the past men who couldn't identify the things they needed to know to do worthwhile things couldn't do them. Of those who learned to learn, some were unable to put knowledge to work to do worthwhile things. Still others didn't develop sufficient expertise to be competitive. Unwillingness or inability to make the transition from "best man" posture to a position in which they could multiply their effectiveness as a manager proved to be a stumbling block for others. Then there were those who proved unable to sense change, spot opportunities, define goals, and develop guidelines. Finally, there were those who couldn't turn ideas into reality.

But, there were also those who could and did do all of these things. Although differing in degree, the pieces of the action revealed that these men learned to learn, did worthwhile things themselves, developed expertise, demonstrated management skills, proved themselves as strategists, and acted as innovators. In short, these men took full advantage of leverage in multiplying the effectiveness of their efforts.

The pieces of the action reveal growth potential early in men's careers. Early indications may show up while a man is still in school if he plays a prominent role in ongoing activities.

Achievement is the measure of the effectiveness of the action. Achievements establish proficiency levels. In the look ahead, the predictive clues pointing to growth or aging are found in the pieces of the action.

The experience of the past reveals that men with growth potential have been the men who have discovered leverage, the men who work smarter not harder. Identify these men to identify those with growth potential.

8

IDENTIFYING MANAGEMENT POTENTIAL

Two EXECUTIVES were having coffee one afternoon in an air-port club lounge. They were waiting to interview a candidate for an opening who was flying in to meet with them. John, the sales vice president, was asking Morris, the personnel vice president, for advice.

"How are we going to really be sure that the man we pick will be a man who can meet the demands of this key management job? I've got two men who have similar backgrounds, education, knowledge, and skills. Both men made good starts as managers, but only one man made the grade over the long haul. Why?"

"That's an easy one," Morris observed, "One had management potential and the other didn't."

"O.K., I'll buy that," said John, "but what is management potential?"

"That's another easy one, John. It's simply having what it takes to develop as a manager."

"Now just a minute, Morris, you haven't answered my

question. All you have said is that of two men with similar backgrounds, education, knowledge, and experience one developed as a manager and the other didn't because one had management potential. Then, you said management potential is 'having what it takes to develop as a manager.' What does it take? That's what I need to know to identify management potential in the men we are interviewing."

"Two things, John, know-how and attitude. First, a man has got to know how to handle himself as a manager. I call this know-how management mechanics. A man must know how to do things such as define the work to be done, delegate, and the like. Second, he's got to look at things the right way. Without the right viewpoint and outlook, a man will never develop as a manager. Attitude controls action."

"Which is the more important, Morris?"

"While both are important, John, I'm more interested in checking on a man's attitude. Know-how is the basis for action, but a man's attitude controls the action. Any man can acquire the needed know-how in a short time, but the men who develop the kind of attitude that gets things done are few and far between."

The search for top talent almost always touches base in the management category. Directly or indirectly, the greater number of searches conducted are for the purpose of identifying management talent of one form or another.

For most positions, it is shortsighted to recruit men who don't have management potential. Few men move very far in an organization before management ability becomes a major determinant of their future progress.

For the most part, men who appear successful as managers are good prospects for advanced positions. But even with their record of success as managers behind them, it's a good idea to take a second look at these men. Some of these men may be trading on technical skills rather than managerial ability. When new and advanced assignments place greater demands on management ability, these men will fail to measure up to requirements.

In the case of men who have traded on technical skills in past assignments, it is doubly important to assess management potentials. Men who have not been called upon to exercise management skills have not had an opportunity to reveal management potential. Yet, the potential of these men may be greater than that of others who have had an opportunity to manage men.

Management potential is more a matter of attitude than know-how. Knowledge of what Morris called management mechanics can be acquired relatively quickly, but the attitude that gets things done takes a long time to develop. Attitude determines man's effectiveness in applying know-how. Attitude is controlling.

Sooner or later, on the way up in an organization many men become stalled and sidetracked. They were good enough mechanics. They missed out, because they didn't have an attitude that permitted them to put their mechanical skills to good use. These men had the needed know-how but didn't look at things the right way.

While there are no hard and fast rules or tests that can be applied in identifying the attitude that reveals management potential, guidelines are available. These guidelines are in the form of "leading" questions.

TWENTY QUESTIONS

In probing the makeup of men, twenty key questions prove helpful; but identifying management potential isn't quite the same as playing the game "Twenty Questions." You can't always be certain of the answers. Yet, in the aggregate, answers to these questions have served as good indicators of management potential.

Reflecting on the mathematics of twenty yes-no questions

is thought provoking. By asking just twenty yes-no questions one can sort a single fact out of a universe of 1,048,576. It's a better than a one-in-a-million ratio. It's like finding a needle in a haystack.

The key questions that serve as guidelines in identifying management potential are questions that must be asked and answered in the minds of managers in assessing a prospect's potential as a manager.

In playing this particular game of twenty questions, you will find the going rough. You can't ask the questions of someone in so many words and expect answers. In fact, you can't ask the questions of anyone.

The questions are thinking questions to be raised in the minds of managers in examining the prospect's record, past and present. Answers to these questions will be revealed in the pieces of the action. The burden, both of asking and answering the questions, falls on the manager who is attempting to identify management potential.

1. Is he actively interested in what others are doing?
2. Does he search out opportunities to exploit?
3. Does he believe that things can be done a better way?
4. Does he believe he could do things a better way?
5. Does he want to tackle the job?
6. Is he afraid of being too late with too little?
7. Is he apprehensive about making mistakes?
8. Does he believe that too many men he must depend on lack competence?
9. Does his dependence on others for assistance and advice worry him?
10. Is he afraid of acting prematurely?
11. Will he accept risk commensurate with rewards?
12. Does he accept full responsibility for final results?
13. Is achievement a source of satisfaction?
14. Is he willing to delegate authority?
15. If it's the best way, will he follow roundabout roads to results?

16. To optimize his achievements, will he make compromises?
17. Is he sensitive to future opportunities he can exploit?
18. Does the outlook appear as promising to him as the past?
19. Does he give up when it is obvious that he can't win?
20. Is he sensitive to detail?

If twenty questions seem too many, remember they are "thinking" questions only. You must tailor them to fit the situation. If a redundancy is evident, it's for emphasis.

THE TIME AND PLACE FOR "YES" MEN

It would be a convenience to all to be able to say, "Give each yes answer five points. Find the man who scores 100."

Unfortunately such numbers are meaningless. However, the experience of the past points to the fact that management potential is equated to yes answers to these key questions. Men assessed as "no" men may be highly skilled in functional specialties but these men lack the outlook and point of view shared by men who have moved ahead as managers.

Men with proven management potential are the "yes" men. These "yes" men vary in their makeup. No two are ever alike. Notwithstanding differences in makeup, men with proven management potential share certain characteristics in common. The key questions highlight these characteristics.

Familiarity with each of these characteristics shared in common by men with proven potential is a must for managers who want to be able to identify men with management potential. Taken together, these characteristics identify the men with high levels of management potential.

1. Curiosity and Interest in the Activities of Others.

The successful manager has been a man who wanted to know what was going on around him in the widest sphere he could encompass. This innate curiosity and interest in the activities of others multiplied his information input. It's been characteristic of him to ask many questions and to listen to the answers given him.

The men who have left their mark in activities in which they have participated weren't raconteurs; they were men who listened to what others had to say. These men point to the fact that they can never have too much information at their disposal. The ideas they exploit and the decisions they make are limited largely by their information input. One executive summed this up by saying, "I've got to continually ask questions and probe. The things I know about I can select or reject, but the things I don't hear about I don't have an opportunity to evaluate and act upon or discard." The best informed men have the best chance of acting effectively.

2. Sensitivity to Opportunity.

Opportunity probably knocks on most mens' doors more than once. The risk men run isn't that they won't hear opportunity knock, but that they won't recognize opportunity's knock when they hear it. Only a few are able to discriminate opportunity's knock from the general background of the rest of the knocking noises heard all the time.

Opportunities aren't obvious to insensitive observers. That's why most men pass them by. We are always surrounded by opportunities. It's only after someone else spots an opportunity and exploits it, that the opportunity becomes obvious to everyone. Relatively simple concepts, such as the electric blanket and the electric toothbrush were consumer product opportunities overlooked by many until someone sensitive to the situation identified them. It's this sensitivity to opportunity that's essential in every area of activtiy in selecting the more worthwhile things to concentrate one's efforts on. As one man put it, "It doesn't take any more effort to do something worthwhile than it does to do some routine job, but you do have to spot opportunities to act."

3. Dissatisfaction with Things As They Are.

Dissatisfaction is a basic ingredient in the makeup of men who are successful managers. The men who get things done are rarely satisfied with things as they find them. Those who are satisfied with things as they are rarely contribute very much to progress.

By itself, as is true of other ingredients in the makeup of managers, dissatisfaction with things alone isn't enough. There are a great many men who just grumble their way through life but don't have the ability to identify things that could be done in a better way.

The chronic complainer doesn't know it, but he gives away valuable ideas. When he grumbles that somebody ought to do this or that, or that they don't make something the way it should be made, he's taken half a step on the road to success. Too many take these half steps, too few take full steps on the road to success.

Dr. Edwin H. Land of the Polaroid Corporation was dissatisfied. It took too long to get photographs. His dissatisfaction led to the development of the camera which gives the photographer a finished photograph a few seconds after he takes a picture. Dissatisfaction is the driving force in the makeup of men who get things done.

4. Conviction That Opportunities Can Be Exploited.

The characteristic that turns chronic dissatisfaction and a sensitivity to opportunity into productive channels is the personal conviction that opportunities can be exploited. It's not enough just to have good ideas; a man must know that these can be put to good use in the future just as they have in the past.

Conviction that opportunities can be exploited comes from recognition of the past experience of others in capitalizing on ideas as well as some understanding of what's involved when one tries to do something new and different. It also involves some appreciation of the ambivalent atmosphere of the land of opportunity. New ideas meet resistance from those who would always do things the way they have always been done. On the other hand there is always a market for new and different products and services once their merit is demonstrated.

When the late Morehead Patterson was head of American Machine and Foundry he, personally, was the moving force behind the successful automatic bowling pin spotter in the face of the unfavorable reaction to the idea expressed by others. He demonstrated a characteristic common to the makeup of successful men, an unswerving conviction that opportunities to do something new and different can be exploited.

5. Decisiveness in Capitalizing on Opportunities to Do Things in New and Different Ways.

Much is said about the ability to delegate as an essential ingredient in the makeup of successful managers, but effective performers do not delegate responsibility for getting new ideas into action. Effective performers accept a personal responsibility to see to it that things get done. They give special attention to new programs because they are aware that new ideas are the ones too often dropped by others when the going gets difficult.

Only those who make decisions to capitalize on opportunities to do things in new and different ways can profit from innovation. Everyone at one time or another has heard someone lament the fact that he thought of doing something long before someone else did it. The comment, "I thought of that a long time ago," points to the man who didn't decide to be among the ones to capitalize on opportunities to do things in new and different ways.

One chief executive commented, "It's my job to take the responsibility for the new things we do. I can hire professionals to do the things that have been done before, and they'll do a better job than I can, but I can't hire the real product pioneers because the men who know how to develop new things are busy running their own business."

6. Apprehension about Acting Too Late.

One of the chief concerns of the effective manager is the fear that he won't act soon enough. He's afraid of missing an opportunity. He knows that he moves forward fastest by capitalizing on opportunities. Good performance on day-to-day activities is important, but the thing that really moves a man ahead fastest is his ability to make the most of opportunities.

Apprehension about acting too late can be considered to be one of the power factors in the makeup of men who get things done. As one man put it, "A lot of times I'd have a better basis for action if I waited a while longer before I acted, but I'd miss a lot of good opportunities. Anyway you look at it the cost of missing a good opportunity has to be balanced against the cost of acting too soon."

The man who is afraid of acting too late will push himself to do more and in a shorter time. He won't waste time. It's the man who feels he doesn't have any deadlines who doesn't get much done.

7. Fear of Failure.

"I seem to spend more time than anyone else around here trying to figure out how to make the least number of mistakes.

In order to get anything accomplished, I have to weigh the consequences carefully, because the problems I create can more than offset my gains. What I try to do is to lay out the different courses of action I can take and then figure out the kinds of trouble I'd get into in each case. Failures are very costly." This one comment does a good job of summing up the thinking of a good many of those with the best records of achievement.

The successful manager is a man who is extremely conscious of a need to avoid failures. However, he admits that he's faced with a dilemma. He can avoid mistakes by doing nothing, but he can't get anywhere on this basis. On the other hand if he tries to move too fast, he may actually lose ground because of the mistakes he makes. Some choose one extreme and avoid mistakes by doing little or nothing. Others run real risks.

The effective performer is the man who plans a mid-course strategy giving careful attention to the exploration of alternative courses of action open to him. To a large degree, his success is dependent on his ability to identify all the different courses he might follow, the one overlooked may be the one that gives someone else a competitive edge.

8. Anxiety over the Plans, Programs, Proposals, and Performance of Others.

"If I had more arms and legs I'd do all of the jobs around here myself," was the comment a corporation president made after a particularly frustrating meeting with his executive committee. This sense of insecurity in what others are doing and the way in which they are working proves troublesome for all highly effective performers. They are aware that their own competence is the result of their disciplined development of knowledge and the thoroughness with which they execute every assignment. They find others lacking in equivalent competence, yet their own personal progress depends to a large degree on the performance of others.

9. Overdependence on Others for Advice, Information, Interpretation, Decisions, and Action.

One manager remarked, "I have the uncomfortable feeling that I don't know what I'm talking about, because the people who report to me don't know what they are talking about." This is typical of the unrest existing in executive suites.

Achievements in every organization are the result of the efforts of more than one man. Too many learn too late that their effectiveness is largely determined by data developed at grass-roots levels in their organizations. Those who are aware of this feel overly dependent on others for the outcome of what they are doing. As one man put it, "The success or failure of the things I do depends, for the most part, on the information, advice, and counsel supplied by others. The only time I exercise much control over things is when I add men to my staff or remove them."

With this degree of dependence on others for success, a feeling of insecurity over the plans, programs, proposals, and performance of others is understandable. Only those who aren't sensitive to the situation could be free of a feeling of insecurity.

10. Concern over Acting Too Soon.

The fear of acting too soon, a characteristic common to top performers, is one which seems to contradict an earlier mentioned characteristic, the fear of acting too late. Top performers worry about both.

If one could wait indefinitely all problems would undoubtedly take care of themselves in one way or another. Few men are offered this alternative. Our educational process is one in which men are trained to search for correct answers. In science and other areas, correct answers are essential to reproducible results. In management matters, on the other hand, the need is to maximize opportunity and this requires action with insufficient information. In a competitive climate few, if any, can wait for all of the data desirable for decision-making purposes. What we try to do is to delay action as long as possible balancing the risk of acting too soon against the risk of acting too late. It's a balancing of the hazards of action based on inadequate data against the probability of missing an opportunity altogether. It's a balancing of one risk of failure against another.

11. Speculator When Risk Is Commensurate with Rewards.

"Gambling can't be considered a dirty word," one executive remarked, "because productive people must take chances all of the time. The difference between gambling in Las Vegas," this executive continued, "and the gamble involved in management decisions is the fact that managers run risks commensurate with rewards whereas in Las Vegas, gamblers play against poor odds."

Any kind of action taken without sufficient information to assure a desired outcome involves risk. Those who move ahead rapidly accept risk taking as part of the price of progress. However, they make every effort to be sure that the payoff of the risk they take is proportional to the risk.

12. Acceptance of Full Responsibility for Final Results.

Those who get things done accept responsibility for final results whether the outcome is a success or failure. "You can move fastest when you're willing to be responsible for the outcome of the things you do. When responsibility is shared, it takes two men to do the work of one man." This comment by one executive sums up the case.

When responsibility is shared, it takes two or more men to do one man's job. When two or more men compete with one man who is willing to accept responsibility for results, he'll be the first to get the job done.

13. Persistence in Pursuit of Results; Satisfaction in Achievement.

The effective manager gets satisfaction from results. Everyone has something that he finds is a source of satisfaction. Men work harder when they are working on something that to them is a source of satisfaction.

High level performers tackle every assignment with equal energy. Their source of satisfaction is found in the final outcome of what they are doing. Low level performers aren't results oriented. They don't derive satisfaction from achievement.

14. Delegator of Authority to Exercise Initiative and Act.

While good producers recognize that they must accept responsibility for what gets done, they recognize that two people can do more than one. They recognize that functional specialization improves performance, too. Most importantly, they recognize that men work best when they are given the authority to act.

Those who won't grant others authority to act penalize their own progress. "I don't second guess competent men," one manager remarked. "The man on the job knows the most about it. He is in the best position to make decisions. Sure, he'll make some mistakes. The chances are I'd make even more than he will. My advice: Put competent men to work. Leave them alone. Two men may do more work than one, but not two heads."

15. Expedient Rather Than Conventional.

"Rules are made to be broken," commented one executive. Procedures are established as guidelines to action. They are designed to serve the needs of the majority of situations. There are always special cases calling for special treatment. Many men fail to understand this.

Results are achieved in the shortest time when action is geared to the needs of the moment. Men who follow rules rarely turn out to be winners.

The top producers recognize that carefully established patterns and procedures don't serve every purpose. They are willing to search out the best course of action and follow it through whatever labyrinth it takes them in achieving results. The long way around may not be the proper way or the shortest way, but it may be the only way.

16. Compromising When Concessions Optimize Achievement.

"I'm after results; I'm not out to prove principles. Some sacred cows must be sacrificed from time to time. It's the end that counts, not the means to the end," commented one executive.

By giving in a little at the right time, you often gain more than by refusing to grant concessions to others. Compromise is cooperation. To insist on having things your own way or not at all isn't selfish, it's shortsighted. Why risk losing everything?

17. Farsighted.

Another word is prescience: Knowing things before they happen. New ideas aren't always good ideas, but unless a man is sensitive to new opportunities he isn't in a position to evaluate and select opportunities to exploit.

Sensitivity calls for selectivity. Real opportunities must be identified. Apparent opportunities aren't all good opportunities. Critical evaluations of risk and reward relationships are called for. Diversification spreads gains and losses; optimism is tempered by caution.

Reserves are part of the picture, too. Without reserves, your sensitivity is dulled. When you lack reserves you can't exploit opportunities, so you fail to seek them out. Top performers always seem to have reserves they can call upon to do more than they are doing.

18. Faith in the Future.

Some confuse faith in the future with optimism but faith in the future reflects a longer range viewpoint than that of an optimistic outlook. Those who have good achievement records have had to invest time and energy over long periods to reap the rewards of longer range payouts. Men who don't have faith in the future pass up some of the best opportunities.

Managers can't demand a day's pay at the end of a day's work. They must be willing to invest time and energy today in programs that they believe will yield a good return in days to come.

In a time when technological complexity is a basic ingredient of so much that is done, the planning, development, and operational phases of programs have necessarily involved longer time periods. Only those who have had faith in the future have been able to participate in longer range programs. Those who haven't had this faith in the future have had to content themselves with shorter and more pedestrian pursuits. These men have paid the price of performing on plateaus having poorer potentials.

19. Realistic versus Idealistic.

Does he give in when it is obvious that he's going to be a loser, or does he battle on against overwhelming odds? Effective managers give in. One executive put it this way, "I'm probably more determined to win a battle than most managers, but when I know I'm going to lose I swallow my pride and concede. My time and energy can be put to better use doing other things. You can't win them all but you can waste time when you won't accept defeat."

The man who won't accept defeat isn't emotionally suited to be a manager. Look at it another way: The man who believes that he is always right isn't emotionally suited to be a manager. Either way you look at it, the meaning is the same.

Persistence up to, but not beyond, recognition of the inevitability of defeat, is a must in the makeup of a manager. Persistence beyond the point where the inevitability of defeat becomes obvious is idealism. It is a disqualifier in assessing management potential.

20. Compulsive Attention to Detail.

"I take care of the big things; the details I leave to others," was the comment of a manager who often found himself in difficulty. On another occasion this same manager observed, "It's frustrating to get good projects under way and then have them fall apart because people don't do the things they are supposed to do."

Successful managers are highly sensitive to detail. They know that they are made or broken by a succession of small things. A careless error in a calculation can destroy credibility. A minor mistake in a report can cause loss of confidence in a proposal. In a manager's day both big things and little things are important. Neither can be neglected.

Details take many different forms. Definitions of work to be done, performance expectations, must be detailed if expectations are to become realizations. Performance inspections must be meticulous; little things count. Three key words in a manager's vocabulary are: *expect, inspect,* and *correct.* To these, add—*in detail.*

ATTITUDE AND ACTION

Men's attitudes control their actions and determine their management potential. This is what Morris was telling John at the airport while they were waiting to interview a candidate for a job. As Morris put it, "Without the right viewpoint and outlook a man will never develop as a manager. Attitude controls action."

When asked for a single word that characterizes the attitude of men who have demonstrated unlimited potential as managers, the only word that came to mind was *dynamic.* But a single word isn't adequate to convey to others the makeup of the what it takes to develop as a manager.

To characterize the attitude of men with management potential, one must use words such as curiosity, sensitivity, dissatisfaction, conviction, and the like. It's still not easy. It is even more difficult to find the men who share these characteristics.

Men with know-how are a relatively common commodity, but men with the attitude that controls this know-how effectively are in short supply—and more difficult to detect.

Part IV

Checkpoints

9

THE COMPATIBILITY AUDIT

MANAGERS must know how men measure up at significant checkpoints. Each assignment places demands on ten critical capabilities in different degrees. A capability profile must be developed for each individual to correct or capitalize on his capabilities. A manager should make such an assessment with the assistance of the individual whose capabilities are being audited. To help managers assure themselves that important aspects aren't overlooked, guidelines are illustrated by a case study.

The personal capability profile shown in Figure 9–1, one completed by Tom Jones of Innovation, Incorporated, suggests a starting point in assessing the capabilities a man commands. Each of the ten groupings in Figure 9–1 covers a capability checkpoint in the following order: drive, responsibility, analytical ability, creative capacity, foresight, communicative skills, technical proficiency, sociability, resourcefulness, and judgment. The questions appearing on the profile are delineative of individual checkpoints. They help men focus their thinking on the pertinent checkpoint.

Figure 9–1

PERSONAL CAPABILITY PROFILE
Tom Jones

Do I know where I'm going?..................................... ~~4~~ 3 2 1 0
Am I a self starter?.. ~~3~~ 2 1 0
Do I see things through?.. ~~3~~ 2 1 0

Do I know what's wanted?.. ~~2~~ 1 0
Do I do what's wanted?.. ~~2~~ 1 0
Is my work done on time?.. ~~2~~ 1 0
Is quantity adequate?... ~~2~~ 1 0
Is quality adequate?.. ~~2~~ 1 0

Do I think things through?.............................. ~~5~~ 4 3 2 1 0
Can I cope with change?................................. ~~5~~ 4 3 2 1 0

Do I do things new ways?.................. ~~10~~ 9 8 7 6 5 4 3 2 1 0

Can I see ahead?.. ~~5~~ 4 3 2 1 0
Do I anticipate change?................................. ~~5~~ 4 3 2 1 0

Can I sell my ideas to others?............... ~~10~~ 9 8 7 6 5 4 3 2 1 0

Do I have the necessary knowledge?............................. ~~3~~ 2 1 0
Are my skills adequate?.. ~~3~~ 2 1 0
Do I know what I'm doing?...................................... ~~4~~ 3 2 1 0

Am I sensitive to reactions of others?........ ~~10~~ 9 8 7 6 5 4 3 2 1 0

Can I identify opportunities?................................... 3 2 ~~1~~ 0
Do I know my resources?... 3 2 ~~1~~ 0
Do I set goals?... 4 3 2 1 ~~0~~

Do I recognize alternatives?.................................... 2 1 ~~0~~
Do I ask for advice?.. 2 1 ~~0~~
Do I run risks?... 2 1 ~~0~~
Do I have the courage to act?................................... ~~2~~ 1 0
Have I defined what I'm trying to achieve?...................... 2 1 ~~0~~

In developing personal profiles, ask the men to make objective assessments of their own capabilities independent of their current assignments. Specific assignments may not demand each of the capabilities at a man's command, but his personal capability profile should reflect each of his capabilities in its relevant relationship to his other capabilities.

Tom Jones, who prepared the profile shown in Figure 9–1,

is sales manager for Innovation, Incorporated, a manufacturer of sophisticated scientific equipment. Tom talked with the man to whom he reported, several of his associates, as well as two men who reported to him in developing this profile of the capabilities he could bring to bear on any assignment he might be given.

For example, Tom was well aware of the fact that he was a highly creative thinker. Those who worked with him were aware of this too. He was continually introducing new ideas and ways of doing things. Even though his current assignment didn't demand a high degree of creative ability, Tom's personal profile reflects this capability in its relevant relationship to his other capabilities.

Tom's profile reveals him to be a man at the top at eight of the ten checkpoints but low at the checkpoint for resourcefulness and at the checkpoint for judgment. His profile presents a good fit for assignments calling for a high degree of ability at checkpoints other than those for resourcefulness and judgment.

From the above example we can see that personal capabilities must first be assessed independently of job demands. Only after you have developed a profile of personal capabilities are you ready to take the next step—to match your capabilities with the demands of the assignment.

Capabilities Jobs Demand

The next step in developing a better understanding of the relevant relationships between capabilities commanded and demanded is to assess job demands.

Again, with the assistance of the man to whom he reported, several of his associates, and two people who reported to him, Tom arrived at the functional capability profile illustrated in Figure 9–2. This profile presents an objective assessment of capabilities demanded by the function performed by Tom.

As revealed in Figure 9–2, the sales manager function places heavy demands on drive, responsibility, resourcefulness, as well as on judgment and average demands on capabilities covered by six of the remaining ten checkpoints.

One of the difficulties encountered in evaluating job demands on capabilities is that of viewing a specific position objectively. It is difficult to separate the job from the man in the job. You need to see the job as it should function rather than see the job as it does function.

For example, a sales manager, having been a former sales-

Figure 9–2

FUNCTIONAL CAPABILITY PROFILE
Sales Manager—Innovation, Incorporated

Checkpoint	Weighting										
Drive	0	1	2	3	4	5	6	7	8	9	*10*
Responsibility	0	1	2	3	4	5	6	7	8	9	*10*
Analytical Ability	0	1	2	3	4	*5*	6	7	8	9	10
Creative Capacity	0	1	2	3	4	*5*	6	7	8	9	10
Foresight	0	1	2	3	4	*5*	6	7	8	9	10
Communicative Skills	0	1	2	3	4	*5*	6	7	8	9	10
Technical Proficiency	0	1	2	3	4	*5*	6	7	8	9	10
Social Sensitivity	0	1	2	3	4	*5*	6	7	8	9	10
Resourcefulness	0	1	2	3	4	5	6	7	8	9	*10*
Judgment	0	1	2	3	4	5	6	7	8	9	*10*

man, may continue to function as a salesman rather than as a manager of salesmen. Under these circumstances, it is extremely difficult to assess the position as it should function to be effective. The sales manager who is calling on customers, preparing proposals, and developing sales prospects confuses any attempt to develop a functional capability profile for a sales manager because he is not functioning as a sales manager.

Frequently, you must ignore what is being done and, to put a position in perspective, develop a functional job description of what should be done and use this as a basis on which to build a functional capability profile. The functional capability profile must reflect capabilities demanded to do the job that must be done. Unless this requirement is satisfied, the profile will serve no useful purpose in determining the degree of fit between capabilities commanded and demanded.

Determining the Degree of Fit

There are two different times when men on the move want to determine the degree of fit between capabilities commanded and demanded. One is when a man wants to improve on-the-job relationships. The other is when a man wants to determine relevant relationships associated with alternative moves he might make sometime in the future.

In Tom's case he wanted to improve on-the-job relationships. He had been in his present position for over two years. Tom wanted to tighten up the fit between his personal capability profile and functional capabilities demanded by his assignment. Having developed the two profiles, Tom was ready to conduct a compatibility audit.

In conducting a compatibility audit, the auditor must be on the lookout for one of three situations. First, the optimum situation is one in which a man commands the capability a job demands at one or more checkpoints. For example, in the optimum situation when the job calls for a self-starter, a man finds that he is a self-starter. The optimum situation is one which reflects the highest degree of checkpoint compatibility between capabilities commanded and demanded.

The second situation, the subcritical situation, is one in which a man's capabilities fall short of job demands at one or more checkpoints. In the subcritical situation, for example, when the job calls for a self-starter and a man finds he isn't a self-starter, someone has to get him going.

Here, the man's capability doesn't measure up to job demands. His drive is subcritical. It's inadequate. Subcritical capabilities fall short of job demands for effective action.

The third situation, the overkill situation, is one in which a man's capabilities far exceed job demands at one or more checkpoints. To illustrate, when a job calls for a self-starter, the man is not only a self-starter but he starts more things than can be carried to completion. The man's capabilities not only measure up to demands but they so far overshoot requirements that his drive is self-defeating and leads to overkill. Overkill negates effective action.

In conducting a compatibility audit, the auditor must compare personal capability profiles and functional capability profiles and determine the degree of fit between the two. Numbers on the profiles serve as thinking tools, but the auditor must go behind numbers and examine, in depth and breadth, capabilities commanded and demanded at each checkpoint.

Optimum Capabilities

Tom, in commencing his compatibility audit, found that his personal capability profile matched his functional capability profile at the checkpoint for drive. Tom repeatedly told members of his staff, "Brownie points are given for results, not efforts. Don't start something unless you can see it through." Tom's job needed a man who combined the driving force of a self-starter with the ability to follow jobs through to completion.

Tom was an excellent match for the function he performed. As sales manager, he was the only one in a position to know such things as what sales calls should be made, how much time salesmen should allocate to each customer, whether or not effective presentations were being made, and when to call off the troops. Tom always stayed on top of the job.

In concluding his compatibility audit at the first checkpoint, Tom noted his findings in the optimum category on the summary audit form, Figure 9–3, before going on to the next checkpoint.

At the second checkpoint, the responsibility checkpoint, Tom again found that his personal capability matched job demands. Tom was well aware that he was the only one who was in a position to know the degree to which he was doing his job the way it should be done.

Tom put it this way, "From a company standpoint the whole monkey is on my back. If I weren't as conscientious about my responsibilities as I am, no one else would know when I wasn't doing a good job. There is no way for them to find out, no way.

"Unless someone takes the time to become as familiar with our markets as I have become and takes the time to do what I am doing, they can't possibly know whether or not I'm doing everything that should be done to build sales as rapidly as sales can be built on a sound basis for profits, stability, and growth in the years ahead."

At this second checkpoint Tom was, again, an excellent match for the function he performed. He understood the meaning of responsibility, and he made use of his knowledge of the nature of responsibility. To Tom and others who know the nature of responsibility it means a willingness to do what needs to be done, the way it needs to be done, when it needs to be done. Anything less is an evasion of responsibility.

Tom was of the opinion that he measured up to these criteria for responsibility in every respect. He was a perfectionist; he placed demands on himself for top performance measured in terms of quantity, quality, and timeliness. Tom classified his findings at the second checkpoint in the optimum category since his capabilities matched job demands.

Overkill Capabilities

The highest degree of checkpoint compatibility occurs when a man's capabilities measure up to job demands. In some situations, men's capabilities more than measure up to

Figure 9–3

COMPATIBILITY AUDIT
Tom Jones—Sales Manager

Checkpoint	*Subcritical*	*Optimum*	*Overkill*
Drive		Self-starter, good follow through.	
Responsibility		Willing to guarantee on-time delivery of desired results in both quantity and quality.	
Analytical Ability			Still weighing the pros and cons after others have acted and won the race.
Creative Capacity			Doing more new things than any program can assimilate.
Foresight			Ideas are too far ahead of the times.
Communicative Skills			Too much, too soon.
Technical Proficiency			Posture of "Ultimate Authority" can't be supported/incompatible with other commitments.
Social Sensitivity			Fitting-in has become an end in itself rather than a means to an end.
Resourcefulness	Fail to combine components into a competitively advantageous relationships.		
Judgment	Lose out to those who balance "rightness" against expediency.		

job demands; they far exceed job demands. This signals a danger point for men because when capabilities men command exceed those their jobs demand, situations are subject to overkill. Too much, too soon can be as bad as too little, too late.

At the third checkpoint, Tom became conscious of his own tendency to overshoot the mark. In talking with one of his associates, Tom remarked, "I know I'm a tiger when it comes to digging for facts, but why use guesstimates when, with a little more time, you can use facts and be right rather than half right."

Tom tried to be among the first to take advantage of opportunities created by change but this posed a particular problem. Doing new things resulted in a need for new facts and figures as a basis for decision making, and the necessary facts and figures took time to develop. By the time Tom had the data he wanted for decision making, others had acted and opportunities were lost forever.

One of Tom's associates told Tom, "You are trying to be too right. You are still weighing the pros and cons after others have won the race. Don't overanalyze things. Be willing to be wrong once in a while rather than 'dead' right."

Tom admitted that this advice made much sense to him. After he had taken time to think it over, he acknowledged that at the analytical ability checkpoint he fell in the overkill column. He also had the uncomfortable feeling that he was headed for another entry in the overkill column as he began to consider the creative capacity checkpoint.

Opportunities to do things in new ways were seized by Tom every time they were brought to his attention. He continually introduced new and better ways of doing things, but others weren't able to assimilate new ideas as rapidly as Tom could introduce them into programs. There was no question in anyone's mind about the ideas Tom introduced. They were good ideas. Yet, Tom knew that they were introduced too fast, faster than they could be assimilated. Reluctantly, Tom faced the fact that at the creative capacity checkpoint he fell in the overkill column.

As he continued his audit, he learned a lesson: There can be too much of a good thing as well as too little. Overshooting job needs can be as serious in its consequences as undershooting job needs.

The lesson he learned continued to haunt Tom as he passed on to succeeding checkpoints. He did have the ability to see things on the horizon. He was able to see them away ahead of others, but too far ahead of others. Time was wasted waiting for markets to catch up with Tom. Sales were lost while customers bought competitors' products that reflected less vision and incorporated ideas more in tune with contemporary thinking. Here, too, at the foresight checkpoint, Tom fell into the overkill column.

The reason why Tom was in the overkill category at one more checkpoint was because of his ability to sell his ideas to others within the company. When Tom had an idea he wanted to put across, he didn't let anything stand in his way until he had sold his idea to others. One man observed, "I didn't like to see Tom coming, because I knew I'd end up buying the idea he was selling and that I would end up regretting it one way or another."

The primary problem Tom faced was the fact that he communicated too much, too soon. He sold his ideas to others before they were ready for these ideas. Again Tom was guilty of overkill.

While the process was painful, Tom was learning things he had to learn. He wanted to improve on-the-job relationships. He wanted to tighten up the fit between his personal capability profile and functional capabilities demanded by his assignment. He was becoming increasingly aware of opportunities to do this as he continued his audit.

The seventh checkpoint focused Tom's attention on his

technical proficiency. Tom prided himself on knowing as much or more about the company's products as anyone in the company. Tom worked many extra hours in trying to maintain his posture as the ultimate authority with respect to the company's products. "That doesn't make any sense to me," Tom's superior commented. "He has a whole group of experts at his command who can answer any questions that are raised. Tom is burning himself out trying to play a role he doesn't have to play."

Tom not only had the knowledge and skills necessary to do his job, there was no question he knew what he was doing, but he was overextending himself in ways which were incompatible with other commitments. It was another case of overkill.

At the next checkpoint Tom was called upon to audit his sensitivity to the reactions of others. Tom had given himself high marks on his personal capability profile at this checkpoint. He made every effort to be "one of the boys" at all times. When bowling was what everyone was doing, Tom bowled. When interest shifted to boating, Tom's face became a familiar face at the marina. He did what others were doing; he wanted people to like him.

Here, too, overkill entered the picture. Tom didn't want to offend people. To avoid hurting a man's feelings, he would let a man continue doing a poor job rather than insist that he "shape up or ship out." Two men often ended up doing one man's job when that man couldn't perform by himself.

As sales manager, it was important for Tom to fit in with others. At the same time, Tom's job demanded that he develop a productive sales group and terminate men who couldn't produce. Any attempt to please everyone was incompatible with job demands. Fitting-in with the group was important as a means to an end. Tom made it an end in itself.

In total, at six checkpoints, Tom's audit resulted in entries in the overkill column. Overkill doesn't result because men's

capabilities are greater than those called for by their assignments. Men should develop their capabilities to the highest
levels attainable. Overkill results when men make use of their
capabilities in a manner which is incompatible with functional
requirements. Tom delayed action because he overanalyzed
situations. He introduced more new ideas than could be assimilated. His ideas were too far out for effective action. He
oversold his ideas. He drove himself to maintain a posture of
ultimate authority in areas where this was not necessary. He
tried to be all things to all people. In short, he overshot the
requirements for effective action as sales manager at six
checkpoints.

The capabilities men command are the building blocks for
effective action in any activity. These building blocks must
be put to use in the manner that best meets the needs of an
assignment. Bridges require building blocks different from
those of a high rise or a dam. A salesman must draw on different capabilities and in different degrees than a surgeon or an
attorney. Tom's overkill at six checkpoints resulted not from a
lack of ability but from failure to draw on different capabilities and to draw on them to the degree demanded by his
assignment.

Subcritical Capabilities

The reason he failed to make effective use of his capabilities
at six checkpoints began to become clearer to Tom as he
commenced to audit the ninth and tenth checkpoints.

Tom wasn't able to identify opportunities. He took advantage of them when they were brought to his attention by
others but he couldn't identify them himself. While he could
look far ahead, take advantage of opportunities others brought
to his attention, and come up with new and better ways of
doing things, he couldn't identify opportunities himself. For

this, he was dependent on others. This proved troublesome, because others didn't always bring him the things he needed.

Tom's inability to size up resources available to him presented him with another problem. Tom didn't know when he was attempting things that required resources greater than those at his disposal. On other occasions, Tom's failure to recognize his resources resulted in unused resources.

Both factors, Tom's inability to identify opportunities and his failure to recognize his resources, made it difficult for him to set goals. Without goals, his activities lacked direction.

Men who want to act effectively must apply every resource at their disposal to the best possible end use. Resources should be noted and evaluated. The strongest combination of resources should be established and the best use for this combination determined. If present assignments don't make full use of resources, an effort should be made to try to modify the existing situation so that better opportunities are provided. Men who do these things are resourceful men.

When men's capabilities don't meet job demands, they are subcritical. Subcritical means inadequate. For example, if the force used in an attempt to move a piano across the room is inadequate to start the piano rolling, applying the force all day will not move the piano one inch.

A man's capabilities are his most important resources. The man who can't combine these components into competitively advantageous relationships can't act effectively.

The man who finds himself in the subcritical category at the ninth checkpoint is the man who isn't putting the pieces of the action to good use. The underlying reason may be found at the tenth and final checkpoint.

Several things were apparent at the tenth checkpoint. First, Tom was fast to act but he didn't act effectively. Getting behind the ball and keeping it rolling is one thing; rolling it in the right direction is something else. Tom failed to take time to explore alternatives before acting. He insisted on doing things the right way. He wouldn't take time to examine alternatives.

In one case, Tom insisted on competitive bids for an essential piece of equipment needed to produce parts for an important customer's order. There were several alternative courses of action that could have been taken. The equipment could have been purchased for immediate delivery without bids. As a second alternative, the parts, available as stock items, could have been purchased.

Tom didn't even consider alternatives. He recognized only one course of action. As a consequence of delays resulting from Tom's insistance on competitive bids, the customer canceled the order.

The second thing that limited Tom's effectiveness as a decision maker was the fact that Tom never asked for the advice and counsel of others. When he had an idea about some new way of doing something, he acted rather than consulted. That is, providing his idea didn't involve running any risk.

Tom did not take chances. While he didn't explore alternatives, he made sure that he thought things through and eliminated risks before he acted. Often, opportunities were lost because of the time Tom took to think things through, but he insisted on having facts. Unfortunately, because he was a one-track thinker and failed to explore alternatives, he found himself doing the wrong thing the right on more than one occasion.

A third factor that clouded Tom's decision making was the fact that, while a man of action, Tom didn't take time to define what he was trying to do. His thinking was centered on action rather than direction. While he could see ahead, anticipate change, and come up with new ideas, he didn't tie these things to any well-defined goals.

Decisions direct the action men take. Everything a man does is determined by decisions he makes. A man's effectiveness is limited by his decision-making skills. As Tom made his last entry in the compatibility audit, he knew the reason why he failed to make effective use of his capabilities at six other checkpoints he had already classified in the overkill column; his judgment fell in the subcritical category.

Tom's compatibility audit, now completed, gave him a basis for action in tightening up the fit between the capabilities he commanded and those his job demanded. At this point it became apparent to him that he should commence work on the two capabilities classified as subcritical. These two, resourcefulness and judgment, were controlling capabilities.

The Facets of "Fit"

The compatibility audit clarifies relevant relationships associated with assignments. Managers, and those who report to them, must be equally concerned with "fit" in capitalizing on manpower capabilities.

No man can be certain of his next assignment. The long-range need is to develop one's individual portfolio of capabilities to the highest degree possible. This permits one to take advantage of the greatest number of opportunities when the opportunity to make a move arises.

No man can ever overdevelop his capabilities; he can only overexercise his capabilities. The effective man doesn't use a sledgehammer to drive a thumbtack into the wall. The effective man has a fully developed portfolio of capabilities. He uses them judiciously. He's ready for the best opportunity open to him.

Index

INDEX